What Is International Business?

Also by Peter J. Buckley

THE CHALLENGE OF INTERNATIONAL BUSINESS

CANADA–UK BILATERAL TRADE AND INVESTMENT RELATIONS (*with Christopher L. Paes and Kate Prescott*)

THE CHANGING GLOBAL CONTEXT OF INTERNATIONAL BUSINESS

FOREIGN DIRECT INVESTMENT AND MULTINATIONAL ENTERPRISES

INTERNATIONAL STRATEGIC MANAGEMENT AND GOVERNMENT POLICY

THE FUTURE OF MULTINATIONAL ENTERPRISE (*with Mark Casson*)

INTERNATIONAL TECHNOLOGY TRANSFER BY SMALL AND MEDIUM-SIZED ENTERPRISES (*co-edited with Jaime Campos and Eduardo White*)

MULTINATIONAL ENTERPRISES IN LESS DEVELOPED COUNTRIES (*co-edited with Jeremy Clegg*)

MULTINATIONAL FIRMS, COOPERATION AND COMPETITION IN THE WORLD ECONOMY

THE STRATEGY AND ORGANIZATION OF INTERNATIONAL BUSINESS (*co-edited with Fred Burton and Hafiz Mirza*)

STUDIES IN INTERNATIONAL BUSINESS

INTERNATIONAL BUSINESS: Economics and Anthropology, Theory and Method

What Is International Business?

Edited by

Peter J. Buckley

First published 2005 by
PALGRAVE MACMILLAN
Houndmills, Basingstoke, Hampshire RG21 6XS and
175 Fifth Avenue, New York, N.Y. 10010
Companies and representatives throughout the world

PALGRAVE MACMILLAN is the global academic imprint of the Palgrave
Macmillan division of St. Martin's Press, LLC and of Palgrave Macmillan Ltd.
Macmillan® is a registered trademark in the United States, United Kingdom
and other countries. Palgrave is a registered trademark in the European
Union and other countries.

ISBN 1–4039–1124–X hardback

This book is printed on paper suitable for recycling and made from fully
managed and sustained forest sources.

A catalogue record for this book is available from the British Library.

Library of Congress Cataloging-in-Publication Data
What is international business? / edited by Peter J. Buckley.
      p.   cm.
Includes bibliographical references and index.
ISBN 1–4039–1124–X
1. International business enterprises—Management.   I. Buckley, Peter J.,
1949–

HD62.4.W57 2005
338.8'8—dc22

                                                              2004052593

10   9   8   7   6   5   4   3   2   1
14   13   12   11   10   09   08   07   06   05

Printed and bound in Great Britain by
Antony Rowe Ltd, Chippenham and Eastbourne

Contents

Notes on Contributors

Mark Casson is one of Britain's most distinguished economists. He has published widely on the economics of the multinational enterprise, entrepreneurship and business culture. In addition to publishing over 30 books in these areas, including *The Economics of Business Culture* (1991), *Enterprise and Leadership* (2000) and *Economics of International Business: a New Research Agenda* (2000), he is currently heading an ESRC-funded project on The History of the British Railway Network 1825–1914. This began in April 2002 and is due for completion in March 2005.

John D. Daniels is Professor at the Department of Management, University of Miami, a past President of the Academy of International Business and Chairman of International Division of the Academy of Management. He is a member of editorial boards of many journals including the *Academy of Management Journal, Journal of International Business Studies* and *Management International Review*. His specialities are strategy formation, implementation and international business. His publications include: *International Business: Environments and Operations* co-authored with Radebaugh, *Relevance in International Business Research, Journal of International Business Studies, Strategy and Structure of U.S. Multinationals: an Exploratory Study, Academy of Management Journal* co-authored with Pitts and Tretter and *Recent Foreign Direct Manufacturing Investment in the United States: an Interview Study of the Decision Process.*

John H. Dunning is State of New Jersey Professor of International Business at Rutgers University, Newark, NJ, USA, and Emeritus Professor of International Business at the University of Reading, UK. He is past President of both the Academy of International Business and the International Trade and Finance Association. He is also Chairman of the Graduate Centre of International Business at the University of Reading and Senior Economic Adviser to the Director of the Division on Transnational Corporations and Investment of

UNCTAD in Geneva. He has been researching into the economics of international direct investment and the multinational enterprise since the 1950s. He has authored, co-authored or edited 40 books on this subject and on industrial and regional economics.

Witold J. Henisz is an Assistant Professor of Management at the Wharton School. His research examines the impact of political hazards on international investment strategy, with a focus on the magnitude of, the technology employed in, and the market entry mode chosen for foreign direct investments. His research has been published in such scholarly journals as *Academy of Management Journal, Academy of Management Review, Administrative Science Quarterly, Economics and Politics, Journal of International Business Studies, Journal of Law, Economics and Organization* and *Strategic Management Journal*. He has served as a consultant for the World Bank and The Inter-American Development Bank and previously worked for The International Monetary Fund. He is currently a principal in the political risk management consultancy PRIMA LLC.

Stephen J. Kobrin is William H. Wurster Professor of Multinational Management at the Wharton School of the University of Pennsylvania. His research interests include globalization, global governance, the social and political impacts of the digital revolution, the politics of international business, and global strategy. Recent articles and book chapters include: *MAI and the Clash of Globalizations*; *Back to the Future: Neomedievalism and the Post-modern Digital World Economy*; *The Architecture of Globalization: State Sovereignty in a Networked Global Economy* and *Electronic Cash and the End of National Markets*.

Bruce Kogut is Professor at INSEAD. Until December 2002, he was the Dr Felix Zandman Professor at the Wharton School, University of Pennsylvania, where he headed the Reginald H. Jones Center. He works in the area of international direct investment, development economics, technology policy and privatization. In June 2003, Peter Cornelius (now senior economist Shell Corporation) and he published an edited book *Corporate Governance and International Capital Flows*, Oxford University Press, which was presented at the 2003 meetings of the World Economic Forum.

Dr Alan M. Rugman is the L. Leslie Waters Chair of International Business at the Kelley School of Business, Indiana University, Bloomington, Indiana, USA, where he is also Professor of International Business and Professor of Business Economics and Public Policy. Dr Rugman has published over 200 articles and 40 books dealing with the economic, managerial and strategic aspects of multinational enterprises and with trade and investment policy. These have appeared in such leading journals as: *The American Economic Review, Strategic Management Journal, Journal of International Business Studies* and *California Management Review*. He serves on many editorial boards and has been a consultant to major private sector companies, research institutes and government agencies.

Daniel P. Sullivan is Assistant Professor of Business at the University of Delaware. His research interests include global strategic management, top management decision making and principles of measurement. His teaching interests include corporate strategy and international business management. He was a finalist for the 1988 Richard Farmer Best Dissertation Award of the Academy of International Business for 'Strategy and Structure in the American Multinational Corporation: the Perspective of the European Regional Subsidiary'. His professional associations include the Academy of International Business and the Academy of Management.

Professor Alain Verbeke holds the McCaig Research Chair in Management at the Haskayne School of Business, University of Calgary, Canada, and is an Associate Fellow of Templeton College (University of Oxford). He has been a member of the European Science and Technology Assembly (ESTA), the highest advisory body to the European Commission on the future of European scientific and innovation policy and has served on the board of directors of various educational and scientific institutions. He has authored or edited 15 books and more than 160 refereed publications, including articles in the *Strategic Management Journal* and the *Journal of International Business Studies*.

D. Eleanor Westney is Society of Sloan Fellows Professor of International Management at Massachusetts Institute of Technology. Her long-term research interest is learning across borders (i.e. how organizational patterns developed in one social context are adapted in other societies). She has authored *Organization Theory and the Multinational Corporation* and *Imitation and Innovation: the Transfer of Western Organization Forms to Meiji Japan*.

Mira Wilkins is Professor of Economics at Florida International University and has spent 40-plus years in academia, having travelled to a total of 63 countries during the course of her career. FIU has honoured her with two awards: for Excellence in Research/Scholarship and the esteemed Professorial Excellence Program award. Her publishing record includes six books she has authored, two books edited or co-edited, and more than 100 articles and reviews. Two of her books have received prestigious national honours, with a number of them having gone through multiple printings and been published in several languages.

1
Introduction

Peter J. Buckley

This volume was inspired by E. H. Carr's *What Is History?* (1961). David Cannadine (2002) in *What Is History Now?* (p. vii) describes that book as 'seminal cum perennial' (but not unchallenged, see *inter alia* Elton, 1967). The book precipitated a debate about the scope, method and subject matter of history. It is my hope that the current book may provoke a similar debate amongst the international business academic community.

It is notable that Cannadine's book contains seven chapters on 'hyphenated history' with the modifiers social, political, religious, cultural, gender, intellectual and imperial. The editor suggests that further 'sub-disciplinary specialisms' could have been added – economic, military, business, local, maritime, art, science, population, family and diplomatic (p. vii). International business has not fragmented. However, it is in danger of being absorbed into 'the functional disciplines of management'. In particular, this is an institutional absorption as business schools (especially, perhaps even exclusively, in the USA) close international business departments in the forlorn hope that this means that the whole of the Business School becomes 'international' or even 'global' in its outlook and orientation. This is largely a myth and represents a retreat from the confrontation of international issues into a safe haven where (usually a single) part of a course, for example on marketing, is designated 'international marketing', likewise finance and other subjects. This, largely American, phenomenon is alluded to in the chapters that follow but given the salience of the USA in the business and business school worlds, it represents a major challenge. Most of the contributors here see an important role for a separate and separable subject of international business whatever the institutional arrangements in universities.

Carr's book led to important curriculum reform in history faculties. The contributors here all have messages for the teaching of the subject, the primary one being the maintenance of the nexus between theory and evidence. The importance of real world data has been central to international business since its inception. The dawning of the importance of foreign direct investment (FDI), largely as a post-Second World War phenomenon, first noticed from the USA and the former imperial powers, led to a growing recognition that the institution that controlled FDI – the multinational enterprise (MNE), needed explanation as an important international institution. The many and varied ways of doing international business required forensic investigation and the fact that many of these utilized cooperative efforts between companies led to a productive phase of examination of (strategic) alliances, joint ventures and technology-sharing agreements. These phenomena, under the collective term 'globalization' – the increased international interpenetration of consumption and investment patterns leading to cultural change and conflicts, the implications of increasing flows of capital, technology and labour across borders and the integration of nation states into economic unions or blocs – all require new forms of analysis. International business is perforce interdisciplinary and in this lies both its immense strength and its weakness in the face of entrenched disciplinary boundaries.

Just like history, international business has changed its methods. History moved from narrative to the search for causation to the search for meaning; from explanation to understanding (Cannadine, 2002, Preface). International business has moved from a primarily economics or single management function approach to an uneasy incorporation of all the social science disciplines focused on its core phenomena. The role of (national) cultures has intermittently achieved salience in this mix and the sociology and anthropology of differences in culture have provided a potent, if sometimes volatile, amalgam with economics in explaining international interactions. Carr said, 'History is a process, and you cannot isolate a bit of a process and study it on its own ... everything is completely interconnected' (quoted by Evans, Introduction to

40th Anniversary edition of *What Is History?* 2001, p. xli). Whilst this is also true of international business, we also have to analyse as well as synthesize.

Again like history, international business has roles for theory (Hicks, 1969), modelling (Hatcher and Bailey, 2001) and practice (Tuchman, 1982). As the contributors here acknowledge, the important factors are the balance and integration between the three. Parkhe (1993) criticized work (on international joint ventures) as non-cumulative and unsynthesized. Such a criticism could be directed against the whole of international business and, although a pertinent point, it would be unfair to a community that takes seriously its philosophical underpinnings and searches for appropriate theory to direct its empirical adventures.

Carr argued that historians were not empty vessels through which the truth about the past was conveyed from the documents to the reader, but individuals who brought their own particular views and assumptions to their work, which had to be read with this fact in mind (Cannadine, 2002, Prologue p. 15). So it is with international business scholars. Just as history should be read as the collective discourse of the historians of a particular time and context, which in turn reflects the times in which they lived, so too has the orientation of the international business community changed. The early pioneers of what became the Academy of International Business (AIB) (founded in the USA) were a group of academics who had a missionary zeal as well as a grounding in management, marketing, finance or economics. The investigation of their interests grew the empirical base of the subject through data-sets and case studies and led to the development of modelling, generalization and theory. The extent of the applicability of theories has been, and continues to be, a source of controversy as is the type of theory most applicable to the mutating phenomena under study. From this emerged (as with history) 'An autonomous discipline with its own specialised methods' (Marwick, 2001, p. 17) and an organized international business profession. The boundaries of the profession, like the phenomena it studies, have changed over time (the decline of finance specialists with the international business community is a puzzle and a worry) and its practitioners have occasionally felt the need to take stock of its position. This book is a contribution to that process (for a final parallel with history see Baron, 1986).

My letter to the potential contributors to this volume included the following three elements:

'I think that the time is right for a fundamental reappraisal of our discipline and hope that this book will be a major part of that reappraisal.'

'The idea of the volume is based on the classic *What Is History?* by E. H. Carr.'

'What I would particularly like is a forceful piece of writing that strongly expresses your opinions on the subject.'

I am glad that I included all these elements. The distinguished group of authors who contribute to this volume generally agree that international business as a discipline requires a rigorous re-examination and they have all responded to the first appeal. Several of them were inspired by the call to parallel E. H. Carr's example and, as you will read, some forceful opinions were indeed elicited!

An inadequate introduction to the chapters

Mark Casson opens the volume with a critical and powerful statement of 'visions' of international business. Six visions are presented: the invisible hand in international business, Coase's vision of planning and markets, the international business system as a spatial network, evolutionary theory, the global information network driven by entrepreneurs and global conflicts between rival visionaries. Casson is concerned with the move from vision (opening up new vistas) to dogma (closing them down through the presence of 'the last word on the subject') and he feels that this is happening rather prematurely in international business. Despite the overwhelmingly critical line, this provocative chapter contains some 'backhanded compliments' to the importance of international business as an intellectual domain.

Steve Kobrin, in Chapter 3, examines the lessons of history for globalization and he emphasizes the 'post material interests' of human rights, cultural homogenization and the environment and their conflict with laissez-faire global policies. The impact of technological change limits the choice of alternative modes of organizing the world economy and constrains but does not determine outcomes.

The contrary material versus ideational pressures on globalization require strong institutions to limit dysfunctional globalization.

Bruce Kogut describes self-referential communities of scholarship which have a shared aesthetic that defines research styles as well as the dynamics of academic labour markets. He sees a strong positive parallel between the dialogue of fact and interpretation that, at best, is the core of the international business field's aesthetic values. In this he finds a parallel with Carr's dialogue between past and present, analysis and facts.

Daniel Sullivan and John Daniels define international business through its research by asking the question 'What knowledge do international business researchers seek, for what purpose and why?' They contrast the scientific perspective with the humanist paradigm and suggest that international business has, up to this point, utilized scientific humanism as its modus operandi. They feel that international business research must evolve from this and see the present (2004) as being an interesting watershed from which international business research will progress.

Witold Henisz examines the institutional environment, especially the local institutional environment for international business, as practised in the current world economy. He focuses on the impact of the institutional context on the strategy of firms and analyses institutional change from both the supply and demand sides. His summary is that although the differences in the nature of business transactions across nations with varying institutional environments have been well integrated and analysed, research on the differences in the nature of business transactions when the supply-side structure of the institutional environment or demand-side forces are likely to generate future change in that institutional environment remains limited.

Alan Rugman and Alain Verbeke (Chapter 7) present a new research agenda focused on 'regional multinationals'. The analysis begins from a specific empirical issue – the unevenly distributed sales of multinational enterprises in individual national markets. The conclusion is that most MNEs stick to their home market in the Triad (North America, Europe, Japan) and that regionalization, not globalization, of sales predominates. The authors pose a big question for future research – why do MNEs succeed as regional organizations without (so far) becoming global? This is both a theoretical and an empirical challenge.

In Chapter 8 Mira Wilkins gives an economic historian's view of 'What is international business?' She gives a succinct overview of key issues and examines the issue of bias in analysis. Her argument is that global economic history is central in the explanation of today's globalizing economy. Normative and policy issues are best handled in the light of historical analysis.

Eleanor Westney gives an account of personal experience in her sociologist's view of the question. She sees a strong parallel between Japanese studies and international business in that both are defined by an empirical phenomenon and share a multidisciplinary approach. The conflict between (discipline based) expertise and specialization versus breadth and integration is evident in the evolution of both academic areas. Both need to make the claim that understanding of their 'central phenomenon' is critical to the portfolio of knowledge and education that their institutional home provides. International business departments as 'keepers of the flame' are contrasted with diffusion of its subject matter to the 'functional disciplines' (distinctiveness versus generalizability is a strategic dilemma for international business scholars). The chapter ends with a strong statement to maintain the 'nexus of the phenomenon and theory'.

The epilogue, by John Dunning, treats international business as an evolving body of knowledge. He echoes the thoughts of others that with the current controversies on globalization, the subject can again become a 'field in ferment'.

These brief paragraphs do not convey the richness and the depth of the individual contributions – there is no substitute, as usual, for reading the originals.

Conclusion

What is international business? The claim that it has become an autonomous discipline with its own specialized methods will not be accepted by everyone. It is a discipline under threat in the USA from institutional changes in most leading universities which are absorbing the subject back into 'the functional disciplines of management', although it thrives in Europe and in the emerging economies. Maybe visions of international business can be pursued even if an autonomous academic community did not exist but then they become much harder to achieve. The world has moved on from the focus of international business as what American companies do abroad to a fully globalized focus on all aspects of business across borders. This is not homogenization. The importance of national, company and organizational culture, the role of language, national laws, regulatory and fiscal regimes, steps towards economic integration into supranational blocs, different spatial configurations of business, consumption and production and the need for innovation, creativity and entrepreneurship (all of which have a local, geographic base) necessitate new lenses of analysis firmly rooted in the notion that business is, and always has been, best analysed as an international phenomenon.

References

Baron, Salo W. (1986) *The Contemporary Relevance of History*. New York: Columbia University Press.

Cannadine, David (2002) *What Is History Now?* Basingstoke: Palgrave Macmillan.

Carr, E. H. (1961) *What Is History?* Basingstoke: Macmillan. Second edition (1967) edited by R. W. Davies, Harmondsworth, Penguin. 40th Anniversary edition (2001), Basingstoke, Palgrave Macmillan.

Elton, G. R. (1967) *The Practice of History*. Glasgow: Collins Fontana.

Hatcher, John and Mark Bailey (2001) *Modelling the Middle Ages*. Oxford: Oxford University Press.

Hicks, John (1969) *A Theory of Economic History*. Oxford: Oxford University Press.

Marwick, Arthur (2001) *The New Nature of History*. Basingstoke: Palgrave – now Palgrave Macmillan.

Parke, Arvind (1993) '"Messy" Research, Methodological Predispositions and Theory Development in International Joint Ventures', *Academy of Management Review*, 18: 227–68.

Tuchman, Barbara W. (1982) *Practicing History*. New York: Ballantine Books.

2
Visions of International Business
Mark Casson

Introduction

This chapter argues that the rise and fall of international business studies over the period 1960–2000 has been driven by the discovery, exploitation and finally a loss of vision in the subject. Six main visions are identified. All of these visions have something important to contribute to IB. But some of these visions have been corrupted, and others have been ignored. Some have been replaced by uninspiring dogmas.

Unless IB recovers its key visions, and nurtures and develops them, it will become marginalized by other disciplines. The intellectual reputation of IB was established in the 1960s and 1970s by visionary writers such as Hymer and Vernon, whose work had significant implications outside the narrow confines of IB itself. IB was quick to take up and develop ideas about economic institutions that originated outside the field, by writers such as Coase and Penrose. But much of this early dynamism in the field has been lost.

This loss of vision is a natural process that has occurred in many fields. Vision becomes less necessary as a field matures, and the precision of formal theory replaces the ambiguity of vision. But loss of vision in IB seems to have been premature. It has happened before an adequate legacy of formal theory has been developed. The legacy of these early visions is not an impressive body of formal theory, but simply a set of uninspiring dogma. The visions need to be recovered, so that further development of theory can take place. Existing dogmas provide useful introductions to the subject, but they are no substitute for proper vision. This chapter sets out the visions that need to be recovered, and considers how the recovery can be attained.

The concept of vision

A vision is a representation of something based upon a mental picture. It typically represents an interdependent system in an abstract form. The system comprises a set of elements and a set of relationships between these elements. In the vision, these elements, and the relations between them, are represented symbolically. A vision is typically holistic – it presents a 'big picture' of the system as a whole. A process of abstraction allows the vision to focus on key relationships, without the distraction of minor detail which would 'clutter' the picture. In some cases, though, a vision may also illuminate smaller parts of the system, particularly when each small part can be pictured as a 'microcosm' of the whole. In other cases there may also be restricted visions, complementing the holistic vision, which picture individual components in greater detail.

The value of a vision is that it summarizes the relationships between the elements in a parsimonious way. A vision also elicits an emotional response when contemplated – for example, it may be said to be 'beautiful' or 'elegant' – and this allows it to be easily memorized, and called to mind when required.

For the purposes of this chapter, it is useful to distinguish between analytical visions, romantic visions and moral visions.

Analytical visions are the main focus of this chapter. They typically employ a high degree of abstraction; relationships may be expressed in geometrical terms, using concepts such as 'symmetry', 'hierarchy', and so on. Many analytical visions represent an equilibrium of the system, and can used to analyse how this equilibrium shifts over time. Analytical visions are important in both natural science and social science. A chemist, for example, may have a vision of how a molecule is built up out of atoms, or an engineer may have a vision of how the links in a transport system can be connected up to form a network.

An analytical vision represents an intermediate stage in the development of a formal theory. An analytical vision corresponds to a theory expressed in intuitive or heuristic terms. After a formal theory has been developed, the vision will normally be retained in order to 'motivate' the exposition of the theory, and to elucidate its scope and limitations.

Romantic visions express the state that a person would like a system to be in. Romantic visions often inspire feelings of awe and wonder. Sometimes the romance is achieved by adopting a particular perspective on a system, such as studying a landscape from a particular angle or in a particular light. There are few books published today on 'The romance of international business', although the Victorians clearly found the discovery of raw materials and the opening up of world trade to be a romantic subject. One of the visions set out below might possibly be described as romantic, but it is probably no coincidence that it is more widely used in geography than it is in IB.

Romantic visions are closely related to moral visions, which relate to states that a person believes that the system ought to be in. Moral visions are discussed in a later section of this chapter. Two main types of moral vision are considered: one that focuses on the value of freedom, and another that focuses on equality instead. These two visions are important because political programmes are usually linked to one or other of these visions. Moral visions are also linked to analytical visions, since many people equate moral Utopias with the equilibrium outcome of a certain types of institutional arrangement represented in some analytical vision. For example, systems based on markets and democracy are said to favour freedom, whilst systems based on planning and the state are said to favour equality. Analytical visions therefore combine with moral visions to make a case for the moral superiority of one kind of institutional arrangement over another.

An analytical vision may be contrasted with a dogma. A dogma is more explicit than an analytical vision. Whilst a vision often represents the 'first word' on a subject, inspiring others to explore it in detail, a dogma is usually meant to be the 'final word' on the subject. If visions are broad, dogmas are often narrow; they become explicit through a process of narrowing down a vision to concentrate on a small number of features which are easy to express. Visions, as the term suggests, are often communicated in pictorial terms, whereas dogmas are usually stated purely in language instead.

A dogma does not have the status of a theory because it is not based upon a logical or mathematical model. It is simply a set of statements which attempt to summarize the implications of a vision, or to outline some (as yet undeveloped) formal theory. It is well known in religious studies that a movement which begins as the result of an inspiring vision often finishes up constrained by a rigid dogma, policed by powerful interests who interpret the original vision in a very narrow way. For example, the original vision may be a form of divine revelation, but the dogma is usually just a carefully crafted form of words, embodied in a creed. This move directly from vision to dogma is most likely when analysing extremely large and complex systems, since they elude any attempt at formal modelling. The global IB system, like the heavenly cosmos, is so complex that satisfactory formal modelling has not yet been achieved.

Vision and personality

Different types of personality may be involved in seeing visions and in creating dogma. Hayek distinguished two personality types: the 'puzzler' and the 'master of the subject' (Hayek, 1978). Visions are disclosed to 'puzzlers', who ponder long and hard over paradoxes, until an ecstatic moment at which the resolution of the paradox is disclosed. At this stage, however, the vision is still rather vague, and much of the detail needs to be worked out. But the 'fog has lifted' and 'the way ahead' is clear. Dogmas, by contrast, are created by would-be 'masters of the subject' – people who believe that knowledge needs to be well organized if it is to spread easily. Not every one has the imaginative capacity to share a vision. Indeed, a 'master' may have struggled hard to grasp the vision and, finding it still elusive, decided to construct the dogma as an aid to others like himself. A dogma has the great advantage that, being codified, it can be learned and memorized by rote. The master of the subject becomes the definitive source from which the dogma flows.

The relationship between the 'puzzler' and the 'master of the subject' is a difficult one. The 'puzzler' is a threat to the master of the subject if he remains active in the field, because he can claim to be the original fount of wisdom, and may attack the master for distorting or trivializing his idea (rather like the conflict between writer and producer when a book is turned into a film). On the other hand, the puzzler may quit the field, having solved the paradox to his own satisfaction, and having thereby lost interest in the subject. He will only return if another paradox emerges, leaving the master of the subject to control the field.

A related distinction, due to Sir Isaiah Berlin, is between the 'fox' and the 'hedgehog' (Berlin, 1953). The fox knows many things, but the hedgehog knows one big thing. The fox resembles the puzzler, and the visionary, because his interests are wide. Nothing is excluded from his view because he is interested in the system as a whole. In this holistic view, everything is connected to everything else; these connections may not be apparent at the outset, but they are there to be discovered.

The hedgehog, on the other hand, takes a more localized view, which means that a single dominant factor can be identified and made explicit. His great insight is the defensive quality of a prickly ball. This is a simple point which is easy to pass on to fellow hedgehogs. He is a natural dogmatist and 'master of his subject' – and he survives remarkably well against attacks from the fox.

Meyers-Briggs personality tests distinguish between 'introverts' and 'extraverts' along Jungian lines. They also distinguish, along a separate dimension, between 'intuitives' and 'sensing' types. Intuitives use mental visions to leap to conclusions, whereas sensing types break down every problem into separate steps and work towards a solution one step at a time. The visionary fits neatly into the intuitive introvert category, because of his preoccupation with developing a distinctive personal view of the system to which everything he experiences can somehow be related. The dogmatist fits neatly into the sensing extravert category because of his desire to formalize his knowledge as a list of separate points. The intuitive introvert finds it difficult to share his vision because he is on a different wavelength from many other people, whereas the sensing extravert knows exactly 'where other people are at', and can articulate his dogma in accessible terms.

The social dynamic of an emerging field of research suggests that in the early stages visionaries will predominate, but as the details of the subject are worked out, masters of the subject will gradually take control. The holistic nature of a vision means that there is only room for a few visionaries at the outset, whereas the more specialized knowledge emerging from subsequent detailed study allows for several masters of the subject to coexist, each concentrating on a separate sub-field. This coexistence is sustainable so long as each master sticks to his own territory, and does not attempt to invade others' territories. Tacit collusion can therefore develop, in which each master refuses to discuss matters connected with another's field.

Serious difficulties arise when dogmatization is premature. An ambitious master of the subject may be tempted to announce a dogma before all the details have been properly worked out. By publicly committing himself to an error, the master provides an opportunity for other masters to invade his territory and take it over. But if dogmatization is premature throughout the field, then masters may be reluctant to attack each other for fear of counter-attack. Collusion then takes the form of a 'conspiracy of silence' – the masters know the limitation of each other's dogmas, but agree not to raise the issues in public. The resulting confusion inhibits intellectual progress, and causes the field as a whole to lose influence, whilst the masters retain their influence within it.

The following sections set out six distinctive visions of the IB system. It is important to emphasize that these visions are concerned with the IB system as a whole, and not just with the structure of an individual multinational enterprise. There are, of course, numerous visions of the multinational enterprise, corresponding to horizontally and vertically integrated firms, unitary and multi-divisional firms, and so on. The kind of vision highlighted in this chapter is not the 'vision' of a 'world class firm' that is used by chief executives to attract customers and motivate employees. There is an enormous literature on 'visions of organization' and the use of vision in leadership, but that literature has a much narrower focus. The 'organization' envisioned below is the organization of the international economy as a whole; if anyone is to be motivated by this vision, it is world statesmen rather than the managers of individual firms.

Vision 1: The invisible hand in international business

The first vision is based on the famous concept of the 'invisible hand', introduced by Adam Smith (1776). Like other philosophers of the Scottish Enlightenment, Smith was entranced by Newton's vision of a celestial equilibrium between natural forces. The Scottish philosophers believed that if only the harmony of the heavens could be reproduced on earth then social progress would be unstoppable.

But what were the social forces whose equilibrium would sustain harmony on earth?

Smith's first attempt at rationalizing social harmony invoked the 'impartial spectator' – a blend of conscience and enlightened self-interest – which discouraged people from antisocial acts and thereby maintained social order. But in the *Wealth of Nations*, the impartial spectator was sidelined, and the discipline of competition was brought to the fore. Buyers no longer trusted a seller because the seller was an upright person, but because each seller competed with others for the buyer's custom. 'Customer focus', and not the impartial spectator, dictated that the seller behaved well. The strategic importance of customer focus derived from the buyer's ability to switch suppliers, which in turn reflected the buyer's access to a competitive market. The market, as an institution, provided a place to which the buyer could go to compare prices; it also provided a system of law, together with standardized weights and measures, which gave him confidence that he would get what the supplier promised him.

Smith believed in domestic competition but not in international competition. Domestic competition would promote innovation and eliminate waste by rewarding producers who could supply more cheaply than others. Systems of production which took advantage of the division of labour to promote specialization would generate cheaper goods and so, through competition, supplant those goods produced by traditional craft methods. In the international sphere, however, Smith was something of an imperialist, and saw no objection to one empire excluding others from access to its supplies of raw materials and labour.

It was the economic theorist and financier David Ricardo (1817) who extended the principle of the invisible hand to the international sphere. He argued that international markets would encourage an international division of labour, in which countries would gain from specializing in the production of those commodities in which their costs were comparatively low. Absolute costs were measured in terms of labour input, and comparative costs were measured by the opportunity cost in terms of the output of alternative outputs forgone.

Ricardo's theory was limited by its reliance on labour as the sole factor of production. When Heckscher and Ohlin studied patterns of interregional and international trade in the 1920s and 1930s they identified land as another important factor. They argued that countries would tend to export those products which used most intensively the factors in which they were comparatively best endowed, and to import those products which used most intensively the factors with which were comparatively most poorly endowed.

The young mathematical economist Paul Samuelson (1948) seized on their ideas, and formalized them using a model in which capital rather than land was the second factor of production. He proved the factor price equalization theorem. This theorem showed that under appropriate circumstances trade in products was a perfect substitute for trade in factors of production. This underscored the miraculous properties of the market: even when factors of production were not tradable, the existence of competitive markets in products would allocate factors in an efficient way.

The 'magic of the market' was highlighted further by the general equilibrium model, popularized by Kenneth Arrow and Gerard Debreu in the early post-war period (Debreu, 1959). The process of competition was reduced to a simple mechanism in which a uniform price prevailed in each market. This price adjusted in response to excess demand; as excess demand increased, price increased continuously. This generated a continuous mapping from the set of today's prices to the set of tomorrow's prices; the mapping had a unique fixed point, which represented the set of equilibrium prices. Trading remained virtual until the set of equilibrium prices had been attained. This competitive equilibrium was socially ideal in the sense that it was impossible making any consumer better off without making some other consumer worse off; in other words the equilibrium was Pareto-efficient.

The combination of the general equilibrium model with Samuelson's variant of Heckscher–Ohlin theory provided the economics profession with a persuasive vision of what a global competitive economy would be like. Competitive international product markets were seen as a guarantor of a global social optimum.

For economic theorists, the population of the world was basically divided into two types of people – economic liberals, who understood the logic of the gains from trade, and the economic theorems which underpinned them, and those who favoured regulated trade, or even autarky, because they remained stuck in the mercantilist thinking which dominated policy prior to Adam Smith. So far as international political economy was concerned, the nations of the world could be classified in a similar way, according to the views their leaders held. Leaders who espoused mercantilism were seen to be impoverishing their own people, as well as the global economy. Democracy was viewed as the political equivalent of the free market, since it gave voters a choice of leader in just the same way as a market gave consumers a choice of supplier. Mercantilist countries, it was suggested, were undemocratic. The elite impoverished the country as a whole by defending the economic rents they earned from factors of production whose value would fall if the country were opened up to trade. The high level of income inequality in some protectionist countries reinforced this view. Once the population understood what was happening they would press for democracy in order to dismiss their leaders from power. A democratic government would liberalize trade, and thereby undermine the rents which had kept the undemocratic elite in power.

This vision remains highly influential to this day. It has proved problematic in IB, however. The pre-eminence of the market in this vision is difficult to reconcile with the practical importance of multinational firms which plan their internal trade. There are many more specific problems too. The immobility of capital between countries in the Samuelson model of trade is difficult to reconcile with the extensive international capital movements characteristic of the modern global economy. The assumption that technology is given, and is everywhere the same, abstracts from the generation and diffusion of technology which is a crucial role of the modern multinational firm. Specific problems of this nature can, of course, be fixed – and have been fixed – but only at the cost of greater complication, or loss of generality elsewhere in the model. To explain the multinational enterprise, a rather different vision of the economic system was required. In this alternative vision the market retains an important coordinating role, but other coordinating mechanisms are introduced as well.

Vision 2: Coase's vision of planning and markets

The market system is so wonderful – at least in theory – that there is hardly any coordination problem that it cannot solve. But what do government planners do? They coordinate resources owned by the state. What do the managers of firms do? They coordinate resources owned by the private shareholders. So why do we need government, and why do we need firms, when markets can do all the coordination that is required?

This was the question posed by a 21-year-old commerce student at the London School of Economics – Ronald Coase. Coase's answer was that we need governments and firms because there are costs of using the market (Coase, 1937). These costs can be avoided by using planning systems. A planning system that supersedes the market is said to internalize that market. Coase's vision was captured most eloquently by Sir Dennis Robertson's (1923) description of firms as 'islands of conscious power in a sea of markets'.

In IB internalization is typically applied to intermediate product markets. Buckley and Casson distinguished two main types of intermediate product. The first is intangible: namely, proprietary knowledge, encompassing technologies, brand names, marketing techniques, accounting techniques and other special managerial skills. Knowledge is a public good, in the sense that it can be shared, although communication may be costly. In a market economy the right of access to proprietary technology can be traded. Such trade is often internalized because of the difficulties of negotiating and enforcing licensing agreements. The internalization of knowledge across national borders generates the high-technology multinational enterprise so characteristic of early post-war US foreign direct investment in manufacturing industries. Internalization can also explain the subsequent multinationalization of knowledge-intensive service industries such as banking.

The second type of intermediate product is tangible: namely semi-processed materials generated within multi-stage production processes. Internalization of markets of this type is exemplified by the 'make or buy' decision. Williamson (1975) initially claimed the frequency of contracting was the key determinant of the make or buy decision, and later amended this to focus on asset specificity instead (Williamson, 1985). There are, however, many other factors influencing the make or buy decision, including the importance of quality control, and the potential savings from rationalization of inventory holding (Casson and associates, 1986, Ch. 3).

Internalization of an intermediate product market can take a number of different forms. Williamson (1975) and Hennart (1982) have suggested that managerial hierarchy, based on authority relations, is the invariable consequence of internalization, but this is incorrect. Internalization can also be effected through internal transfer prices set by negotiation between the managers of different activities within the firm. In the sharing of knowledge between subsidiaries, for example, the multinational firm may resemble a collegiate members' club.

Although the primary focus of internalization theory is on intermediate products, it has important implications for labour markets and capital markets too. As Coase pointed out and Simon (1957) later emphasized, the employment relationship, in which workers agree to accept the authority of management over the direction of their work, is a form of internalization of labour services. In a similar way, a diversified conglomerate firm, which allocates investment funds between different divisions, effectively internalizes a capital market. In the absence of the conglomerate, each of the division's activities would be independently owned and each would be separately funded through the external capital market.

Both government and firms use planning systems, but with this important difference – that government itself decides what the scope for planning is to be, whilst the market determines which activities firms are allowed to plan. In deciding which firms are to internalize which activities, the capital market has a crucial role. A firm is profitable when its planning activities supersede very costly market operations, but a firm which supersedes cheap and efficient market operations is likely to make a loss. The capital market makes judgements on which forms of internalization are likely to improve efficiency. When market sentiment favours internalization, a merger and takeover boom is likely, whereas when sentiment is against internalization, divestments, management buy-outs, and start-up funding for small firms will be favoured instead.

Mistakes will, of course, be made: when the gains from internalization fail to fulfil their promise, a firm may close down, or be broken up, and coordination will return to the hands of the market; conversely, when the gains from internalization exceed initial expectations, the firm will grow. In the world of internalization, therefore, the market still 'rules', in the sense that market forces dictate which markets are internalized and which are not. But the market that rules is a costly market, and not a perfect market, and it is used only because it less perfect than an alternative planning system.

Vision 3: The international business system as a spatial network

Coase was not completely explicit about the nature of the costs of using the market. He mentions the cost of discovering prices, which suggests that he regarded lack of information as the principal problem. Information problems are often tackled by intermediation rather than by internalization. Intermediation is occasionally effected by brokers – as, for example, in the housing market – but more usually by middlemen who buy and resell products. To pursue the logic of Coase's argument further, intermediation must be taken fully into account (Casson, 1997).

Consumers suffer from acute information problems, since they purchase a wide range of products, many of them on an intermittent basis, and so intermediation is crucial in the distribution of consumer goods. To reduce consumers' information costs, retailers stock an assortment of products which consumers can inspect and purchase on demand. Retailers assemble their assortments by purchasing from wholesalers, who in turn procure their supplies from producers. Retailers typically agglomerate in urban centres so that consumers can easily compare the prices in competing shops. Neighbouring urban centres vie to attract consumers by offering the strongest competition in the widest range of products (Dicken, 1998).

Wholesalers need to deliver to many different urban centres, which requires them to locate at nodes on transport networks, such as motorways or rail hubs. Break of journey is costly where transport is involved, and so to minimize the overall disruption to journeys, warehouses are often concentrated at points where break of journey has to take place in any case. The classic example is ports, where consignments are trans-shipped, or switched to another transport mode. Just as retailers tend to agglomerate in urban centres where major populations of consumers are to be found, wholesalers tend to agglomerate at road and rail intersections, and major ports.

In industries where products are standardized and mature, and are produced using continuous flow technology, wholesaling is a fairly routine activity. The same pattern of consolidation ('making bulk') and distribution ('breaking bulk') repeats itself each period. But in industries with continuous product innovation and small-scale batch production, matching supply to demand on a continuous basis requires a change of plan every period. Wholesaling therefore requires sophisticated management skills.

Wholesaling is important not only for the distribution of consumer goods, but for the distribution of intermediate goods as well. In a multi-stage production process, wholesaling is particularly important when demand is volatile and batch production is used to provide flexibility. Wholesaling is common in industrial districts where merchants subcontract production at each stage. Wholesaling permits an agglomeration of small independent factories in an urban neighbourhood. It sustains a system of 'flexible specialization', which is more efficient than a single large vertically integrated factory (McCann, 1998).

Discovering prices is important in factor markets too. Banks play a crucial intermediating role in the market for capital. They effect maturity transformation by collecting short-term deposits from millions of savers, and lending their funds long term for commercial investment.

Manpower agencies resell labour services, and recruitment agencies broker job placements. To assure competitive wages, and continuity of work, employees like to be able to change jobs without relocation. This calls for a wide range of local employment opportunities, which in turn encourages the concentration of industries demanding similar skills in the same location. This is one of the most important factors in the agglomeration of R&D. Scientific research is a highly specialized activity, and many research scientists avoid relocation because it may disrupt their children's education or their spouse's professional career. To attract good scientists, firms locate their laboratories close to those of other firms who require similar skills. Access to local universities for basic research may also be a factor in agglomeration, although a good supply of graduates may be just as important too.

Warehousing is a space-intensive activity, which therefore tends to force out other activities from a location. Intensive traffic movement at warehouse centres may generate congestion and reduce quality of life. Many R&D centres seem to keep their distance from warehouse centres for this reason, despite the fact that the travel facilities afforded by warehouse centres are often good. Manufacturing tends to take place on marginal land which is unsuitable for other activities. Other things being equal, this location strategy keeps costs of production down, although if manufacturing is too remote from warehousing then its advantage will be eroded by higher transport costs.

These considerations lead to a vision of the IB system as a spatial hierarchy. The key points in the hierarchy are great wholesale centres, where products are collected from manufacturing centres, graded and sorted, and despatched to urban centres of consumption. Historically, changes in transport technology, allied to major infrastructure investment, have determined how the number, size and location of these great centres have evolved. In medieval times the principal metric in economic geography was nautical distance. In the nineteenth century, railways provided a new metric, while in the twentieth century the motorway became paramount. Perhaps in the twenty-first century, the cost of moving goods by air will determine the location of new industries. It is not only technology, however, but also public policy, that influences spatial structure in IB. Thus the liberalization of trade through reductions in tariff and non-tariff barriers has reduced importance of national distribution centres; in Europe, for example, the Benelux countries have achieved unprecedented importance in the hierarchy of distribution as distribution has been rationalized on a Europe-wide basis.

Vision 4: Evolution

Evolutionary theory has become extremely fashionable in social science. Most evolutionary thinking is based on the 'behavioural' view that people are programmed to follow specific patterns of behaviour. Some writers postulate that programming is genetic, whilst others consider it to be cultural. Evolutionary models in IB typically adopt the cultural view, in which socialization within the firm's management team programmes managers to act in a distinctive way. The programming is perpetuated as each new generation of recruits assimilates established routines.

In neoclassical models of IB, the system adjusts to changes in the business environment by managers adapting corporate strategies to new conditions through rational choice. In evolutionary theory by contrast, adjustment occurs mainly by selection. Firms with appropriate strategies survive, and those with inappropriate strategies fail. Competition selects the fittest, and the fittest firms are those which use the most appropriate strategies.

Dynamics plays a crucial role in evolutionary models. There is a given set of possible strategies, and initial conditions specify the number of firms pursuing each type of strategy. Once the system starts running, competition eliminates certain types of firm, and so alters the competitive conditions prevailing between the remainder (Hannan and Freeman, 1989).

Many evolutionary models focus upon a single industry, rather than the business system as a whole. They track the composition of the population of firms in order to provide a 'moving picture' of the dynamics of the industry.

If the environment is stable then the system will tend to converge towards an equilibrium in which a relatively small number of firms all pursue the same efficient strategy. The long-run implications of the model do not therefore differ materially from those of a conventional model of rational choice, in which all firms would make the same rational decision. Indeed, the final equilibrium on which the system converges may well be independent of initial conditions, just as in a conventional model of rational choice.

The distinctive results obtained from evolutionary models often arise from assumptions of economies of scale and scope. Firms do not simply compete on price, it is assumed, but rather compete for market share. This generates non-linearities in the system. Firms with large market share are able to spread their fixed costs further and so are able to undertake more R&D. Greater R&D leads to faster innovation, which drives down a firm's costs relative to those of its competitors and thereby fuels its further growth (Cantwell and Iammarino, 2003).

Non-linear systems often have multiple equilibria, rather than the unique equilibrium characteristic of models of perfect competition. With a multiplicity of equilibria, some of the equilibria will be unstable; a small disturbance of the system will cause it to move away from one equilibrium and towards another instead. The evolutionary path may become highly sensitive to initial conditions; in extreme cases, chaotic behaviour may result, whereby a tiny change in initial conditions leads to a radically different evolutionary path.

Evolutionary writers usually claim to work in the tradition of Joseph Schumpeter (1934), who highlighted the role of major technological innovations in the progress of the economy. Although Schumpeter was certainly a visionary, his vision encompassed the entire evolution of the international capitalist system, beginning with the growth of Italian banking in the thirteenth century (Schumpeter, 1939). It also included other sources of progress besides technology, such as discovery and colonization, and the development of the monopolistic trust.

The most obvious precursor of the evolutionary vision in IB is not Schumpeter, but Hymer (1976). Hymer's doctoral dissertation prophesied the emergence of global oligopolies in high-technology industries. Its emphasis was on the growing spread of multinationality, and the increasing concentration of global economic power, providing a distinctive evolutionary vision. It is perhaps unfortunate that Hymer subsequently compromised his vision with a public commitment to Marxist dogma – a dogma that was too rigid to allow him to develop the full potential of his approach. His premature death was an even greater catastrophe, since had he lived he would almost certainly have contributed much to the refinement of the evolutionary vision of IB.

Vision 5: A global information network driven by entrepreneurs

A significant advantage of the evolutionary approach to IB modelling is that it allows for different firms to behave in different ways. A weakness of the approach, however, is that each firm is programmed so tightly that it is constrained to behave in just one particular way. Conversely, the advantage of the neoclassical approach is that all firms adapt to change, while its disadvantage is that all firms adapt in exactly the same way.

To get the best of both worlds, it is can be postulated that, while all firms can make choices, the strategies that they actually choose will vary from firm to firm. There are several reasons why choices may differ. Some decision-makers may recognize strategic options of which others are not aware. Some managers may have access to data that other managers lack. Finally, some managers may employ different mental models of the environment, so that they interpret the same information in a different way.

One factor unites all of these possibilities – namely unequal access to information and knowledge. A central point in the early work of Hayek is that information is unevenly distributed throughout society.

Sources of factual information are often localized, so that people 'on the spot' get to know about key events before everyone else. According to Hayek (1937), the market system provides incentives for people to specialize in collecting privileged information ahead of others. They can take up speculative positions in markets to exploit their information. People who specialize in seeking out information in order to identify profit opportunities may be termed entrepreneurs. Communication of information is the focus of this vision, and the key actor is the entrepreneur.

Most long-term investment decisions are entrepreneurial in the sense that they benefit from access to superior information and knowledge. The success of an investment decision typically depends, not upon a single item of information, but upon a synthesis of different items of information from different sources. This synthesis is effected with the aid of a mental model, and the success of the decision will depend not only on the accuracy of the information but upon the quality of the model.

An entrepreneur cannot be in several places at once, and so much of the information that he uses must be obtained at second hand. The communication of information is therefore crucial to entrepreneurial activity. It is a truism that technological innovations such as the telegraph, telephone and the internet have accelerated communication. More significantly, they have reduced distance-related costs relative to other costs, and thereby promoted the globalization of communication. The social dimension of communication must be recognized as well. Social networking is a useful way for entrepreneurs to tap into diverse sources of information. The social groups in which they network will also influence the types of investment strategies they consider, and the types of mental models that they employ to evaluate them.

Entrepreneurs take major investment decisions only on an intermittent basis. Much of their time is spent dealing with short-term shocks of a relatively minor nature, such as transitory fluctuations in consumer demand. These minor shocks can be dealt with using routine procedures, and for this purpose the entrepreneur will establish an organization whose members are delegated to carry out the relevant routines (Casson, 1997). The link between the initial investment decision and the subsequent routine demand for information processing connects entrepreneurship to the organization of the firm. It shows that the foundation and growth of firms are intimately connected with the information structures of the economic system. While elite social networks handle commercially sensitive information about major investment opportunities, routine telecommunications handle the daily information required for the organization of production and the conduct of trade.

This vision of IB as an information system supporting the activities of entrepreneurs is complementary to vision 3 above. Instead of focusing on movements of products and the people, it focuses on the movement of information. The entrepreneur strives, in effect, for cognitive competitive advantage. He exploits communication networks strategically to achieve a unique synthesis of information. The successful entrepreneur takes a wider view of the situation than other decision-makers. He may formulate strategies that others overlook, he may identify new markets that others have missed, or he may be the first to recognize a new technology that is ready to be exploited. While everyone takes rational decisions, entrepreneurs consider wider options, using information from wider sources, and using mental models which provide them with a wider view of the situation. Many of the large multinationals of today can trace back their ancestry to small firms founded by entrepreneurs several generations ago.

Vision 6: Global conflicts between rival visionaries

All the visions so far assume that rivalry and conflicts are mediated by some sort of institutional framework. They all agree that markets of some sort contain conflict within a framework of rules. Rival firms do not burn down each other's premises, or attempt to assassinate each other's executives. Moreover, all the visions assume that the basis of conflict is mainly just a selfish desire for greater access to scarce resources.

It must be recognized, however, that people derive enormous satisfaction from the visions that inspire them. This is particularly true of the moral visions discussed below. But it also applies to analytical visions of the kind discussed above. Some political leaders believe passionately in the value of markets in supporting individual freedom, for example, and so derive great emotional reward from contemplating the vision of the invisible hand. Other political leaders, however, believe that there is significant irrationality in people's behaviour, and that without state intervention the economy may spiral out of control. Such politicians derive substantial emotional reward from contemplating the evolutionary model, because its chaotic tendencies legitimate the interventions they are predisposed to make. There is, therefore, a powerful synergy between moral visions of the state the IB system ought to be in, and the analytical visions describing what state the IB system has a tendency to be in. Analytical visions are promoted by politicians who believe that they can help to legitimate a policy which has been devised with a particular moral vision in mind. This combination of moral vision and analytical vision may be termed an ideology.

If these ideological conflicts were resolved purely by means of the market, then the politicians on each side would set out to raise funds from their supporters in order to buy off the opposition. They would form a club, or 'party', which would raise funds to compensate people who would stand to lose out from their policies. This market solution resembles, to some degree, a 'corrupt' election, of the sort that could be found in, say, eighteenth-century England.

But a political leader with a moral vision that cannot be attained with the aid of a market may well decide to pursue his vision by other means. He may decide upon war, terrorism or sabotage. If his military power is very great, the mere threat of force may induce his rivals to make concessions. If rival leaders are purely selfish, they are unlikely to go to war unless there is a difference of perception over who is likely to win. Wars occur when one or more of the parties overestimates their own power, and so expects an easy victory which the other party will not readily concede.

A moral visionary may go to war even if he believes that he is likely to lose. Unlike a selfish leader, his aim is not to plunder resources, but to put an end to the evil perpetrated by his rival. He may resort to extreme methods, because he is happy to destroy his own resources, as well as those of his rival, in the process. Ideological rivalry of this sort can therefore lead to Armageddon.

When a moral visionary opposes a selfish leader, the visionary will obtain strategic advantage because of the credibility of the threats that he can make. If the selfish rival knows that the visionary is prepared to commit all his own resources to the fight, then he knows that he may have to commit all his own to match them. He knows, moreover, that his superior military prowess will not deter the visionary so long as the visionary knows that his rival's victory will only come at a terrible cost in terms of resources actually used. Under these conditions, the selfish leader has a strong incentive to come to terms with the visionary leader if he can. But the only terms acceptable to the visionary will be a change in the selfish leader's moral behaviour.

This vision of conflict between visionaries casts doubt on the long-term political stability of the IB system. Such instability is consistent with the decline of empires in the past. Mature empires governed by long-standing ideologies have been undermined and eventually destroyed by attacks from outsiders imbued with inspiring moral visions (and sometimes by internal revolutionaries too). The visionaries have resorted to violence in order to 'liberate' people from subjection to decadent elites, or to destroy hated cultural artefacts that express a rival vision.

On the other hand, it could be argued that modern global capitalism is relatively stable because it has effectively eliminated the moral visions that would drive people to war. In the post-modern world, it may be said, there are no longer any grand visions worth anyone dying for.

The only moral vision that is taken seriously by the secular liberal elites which govern most Western countries is the right of the individual to be 'free'. On the face of it, this is rather surprising, since freedom, is not, of itself, a very inspiring vision. James Buchanan (1979) sees the value of freedom in the 'right to become the person I want to become', whilst others see it in terms of developing natural abilities or simply 'expressing oneself'. Not only is the vision very local and personal, but it is also very unclear what the result of all this personal exploration is likely to be. It does not seem to afford the same degree of inspiration as, say, participation in committed teamwork directed to a common social goal.

The other dominant vision in the twentieth-century West has been the pursuit of social equality. This vision has faded in recent years, however, because it is considered increasingly impractical, and a serious impediment to national economic growth. The pursuit of equality, it is now believed, extracts a heavy penalty in terms of both freedom and material prosperity. This cynicism and despair about the viability of traditional moral visions keep most Western nations committed to the pursuit of freedom and prosperity through the market.

Evaluation of the visions

If IB were a vibrant discipline, the relative merits of these alternative visions would be fiercely debated. As it happens, very little debate of this nature occurs either at conferences or in the journal literature. Where debate occurs, it generally takes place on methodological grounds. The issues centre on statics versus dynamics, rationality versus behaviourism, and equilibrium versus disequilibrium.

A long-standing criticism of the general equilibrium model is that it is inherently static, and therefore incapable of explaining the evolution of the IB system over time. The static nature of the general equilibrium model derives from the fact that there is a unique equilibrium set of prices, and that prices converge on this equilibrium independently of initial conditions: what ever the initial prices, the final equilibrium is always the same. This does not mean, however, that the model cannot explain changes over time. If tastes, technology or factor endowments change then equilibrium prices and quantities will change as well. Using 'comparative statics', the general equilibrium model traces back the effects of changes in the patterns of trade and investment to underlying changes in tastes, technology and endowments.

It is not only the physical distribution of factor endowments which is important, but their ownership too. Foreign ownership of capital, for example, implies that profits will accrue to foreign consumers, whose tastes will then carry greater weight in the allocation of resources in production. The general equilibrium is therefore conditional upon the way that ownership is distributed. A general equilibrium is only socially optimal once the distribution of ownership is taken as given. There are, therefore, as many different social optima as there are different patterns of ownership. The model has nothing to say on the crucial policy issue of whether a redistribution of ownership would improve global welfare.

The same criticism of being static is often levelled at the Coasian vision too. This criticism, however, ignores the fact that Coasian theory applied to IB highlights the internalization of propriety knowledge. A firm's commitment to exploit the results of its own R&D links its *growth* of production to the *level* of its R&D activity, and so accounts for the growth of the firm. It is, however, only steady-state growth that is explained in this way, and so the static nature of the theory still remains to some degree.

The spatial network vision of IB is also static in the sense that it explains the structure of the spatial network in terms of the current demands that are placed upon it. It is, however, very well placed to explain the long-term historical changes in the spatial structure of IB in terms of the growth of world population and income, and the development of new transport technologies, particularly the steam engine, the internal combustion engine and the jet engine.

Evolutionary theory, as its name suggests, claims to be more dynamic. This claim rests largely on the fact that it analyses out-of-equilibrium behaviour. In evolutionary theory the process of adjustment takes so long that it is this process itself, rather than a change in the underlying equilibria, that explains the changes in the system. However, by implicitly downgrading the importance of external changes in tastes and factor endowments, evolutionary theory overlooks some important aspects of change that are successfully explained through comparative static analysis.

The most satisfactory way of explaining historical change is to combine the effects of changes in the equilibria and changes brought about through the process of adjustment. The vision of a global information network goes a significant way towards achieving this objective. The global network channels information to entrepreneurs, whose individual responses, in the aggregate, lead to price adjustments which update the equilibrium of the system as changes occur. Changes in the system therefore reflect the underlying changes which are being monitored, together with the speed and accuracy with which entrepreneurs respond to change.

The final vision is very different from the others. It offers a very different picture of the prospects for the global economy. It identifies a new strategy – violence – backed by a new motive – the implementation of a powerful moral vision. It is not fundamentally different, in methodological terms, from the other vision; it is simply that the preferences of individuals are moral rather than selfish, and the range of strategies is wider because the constraint of always resolving conflict through the market has been relaxed.

Dogma versus debate

It is interesting to note that this final vision could, in principle, be applied to analyse conflict between rival visions in IB. If IB academics were as inspired by their analytical visions as political activists are by their moral visions, then the IB profession should be locked in violent conflict over the merits of alternative visions. Hopefully the violence would be purely verbal. Proponents of one vision would seek to identify flaws in their rivals' visions, and mercilessly expose them at conference debates. The profession would agree certain ground rules which would keep debate orderly.

In practice, such rules are completely unnecessary because debate between rival visions almost never takes place. When it does, it is usually linked to arcane points of methodology rather than to live policy issues. Potential conflicts over the relative merits of inspiring visions have been largely supplanted by the marketing of simple dogmas. There is not even much direct competition between one dogma and another. Each dogma attempts to dominate some specific area of the subject, and avoids conflict with the dominant dogmas in other areas. There appears to be little interaction – either personal or professional – between the chief proponents of these different dogmas.

While there are several dogmas in IB, it is convenient for the purposes of this chapter to focus on those which grew most directly out of the visions reviewed above. The discussion will therefore concentrate on Dunning's eclectic theory (Dunning, 1977) and also Williamson's transaction cost theory. These are appropriate choices because they are also two of the most influential dogmas in IB.

The first generation of economic theorists in IB, writing in the 1960s, relied heavily on the general equilibrium model. But it proved difficult, using this model, to distinguish between direct and indirect (or 'portfolio') investment flows. The Coasian vision, introduced to IB in the 1970s, addressed this issue head on. But the power and generality of the Coasian vision were undermined by Dunning's eclectic theory when, in its initial version, it associated internalization almost exclusively with technology transfer. Coase's theory, it was said, explained why the 'ownership advantages' of multinationals were 'internalized'. This reduced Coase's general theory of organization to a specific theory of the licensing decision. Thus Coase's insight was neutered so that it could be fitted neatly into the emergent dogma of the 'eclectic theory'.

Another modern Coasian dogma is promoted under the label of 'transaction cost economics' or 'the new institutional economics'. Here Coase's insight is, allegedly, combined with insights from behavioural economics, due to Simon, and from traditional ('old') institutional economics due to Commons. Coase's general concept of 'planning' is equated with managerial hierarchy, while his concept of the 'cost of discovering price' is reduced to dealing with 'hold-up' problems. In both cases an initially broad, but admittedly vague, concept is reduced to a single narrow, but more explicit, concept.

Just as with the eclectic theory, the subject to which the insight is applied is dramatically reduced in scope. Coase's original insights related to the economy as a whole – he operated at the same level of generality as general equilibrium theory. But transaction cost economics, as its name suggests, focuses on the individual transaction. This transaction, moreover, is usually identified with a transaction between an upstream producer and a downstream producer in a multi-stage production process. It is this narrow focus which is partly responsible for narrowing down the concept of 'discovering price' to dealing with the 'hold-up' problem. The net effect of all this is that Coase's original insights are now expressed in two differing dogmas, neither of which does justice to his original vision.

With respect to the other visions discussed above, very few of their insights appear in either of these two dogmas. The net effect, therefore, is that a single vision is split into two dogmas, neither of which includes many of the insights from other visions of IB.

Explaining the loss of vision

It is not the object of this chapter to allocate blame for the loss of vision, but it is nevertheless relevant to speculate on underlying causes. To some extent, loss of vision in a subject is a natural consequence of its maturity, as noted above. A mature subject develops formal models which give clarity to issues on which a vision may be ambiguous. But IB has not matured in this way, and in this sense the dogmatization is therefore premature.

It would be easy to condemn the IB profession for intellectual laziness, and to ascribe this laziness to the incentive structures under which researchers operate. Competitive pressures for promotion, driven by job insecurity, produce a focus on crude productivity measures such as publications. The appreciation of vision is a reflective, and therefore time-consuming, activity, which is easily driven out of a busy person's schedule. Furthermore, the easiest papers to write are those that build on well-known dogmas, rather than those that reflect on visions appreciated by only a few.

It would also be possible to blame the contemporary culture for the loss of vision. Previous generations were accustomed to working with very grand visions of society, from the idealistic visions of the world's great religions, to the political visions associated with liberalism, socialism and nationalism. Both business leaders and their critics would draw freely upon these wider visions in order to debate the legitimacy of business activities. The present cultural climate, however, in which a highly secular form of liberalism has become the dominant ideology, offers nothing very dramatic in the way of social visions. Visions have become more local and personal, as explained below.

It could be said that dogmatists, or 'masters of the subject', are a natural target for blame, but this would be grossly unfair because there is clearly a strong demand for their products. If the existing dogmas did not exist, worse ones would almost certainly take their place. If dogmatists controlled the editorial processes of leading journals, there is clearly a risk that they would abuse their power by criticizing anyone who attacked their work. This is a minor concern, however, because, on the whole, leading dogmatists do not edit leading journals. Problems can arise, however, when editors allow the dogmatists to 'vet' their critics by inviting them to referee their critic's work under the cloak of anonymity.

The inherent complexity of the IB system may explain the lack of progress in formal modelling, but this cannot be the entire explanation because there have been significant innovations in formal modelling which have not been taken up in IB. Lack of mathematical training in recruits to IB research may be part of the problem. The origin of IB in the study of business and foreign cultures may have given an 'arts-based' bias to the subject. But if this were the case, it would be expected that vision would retain an important role in the subject.

The influence of consultancy and management education may also be a factor. It is possible that it distorts academic incentives in business schools. It is noticeable that other management subjects, in addition to IB, suffer from premature dogmatization. Perhaps the short-term horizons and need for 'quick fixes' give managers a strong preference for dogma. Some academics may be obliged to teach in a dogmatic style to obtain good reports from weaker students, and this may spill over into their research. Analytical vision would be too difficult and time-consuming for many students to assimilate.

While *analytical* vision may not be popular with certain types of business school student, however, there is little doubt that *romantic* vision is highly valued. These romantic visions are, however, focused on the individual firm rather than the IB system as a whole. It may seem paradoxical that at a time when grand social visions have lost their power, the visions of business leaders have become highly valued. The paradox is easily resolved, however. The loss of social vision means that 'vision' may be acquiring scarcity value. Secular liberalism encourages people to formulate personal visions of a local nature. Some of these are very trivial, such as consumer 'lifestyle' visions which can be implemented simply by redecorating the house. Grander personal visions often centre on founding a firm, and this has turned the start-up entrepreneur into a role model. Fantasies about the dramatic growth of their start-up firms seem to provide immense satisfaction to large numbers of people.

The importance of vision to the entrepreneur is underlined by the claim that vision is not only a source of intrinsic satisfaction, but an instrument of growth, because it is a motivator for employees (especially those who have no significant personal visions of their own). In the past, founders of firms could free-ride on the social visions promoted by political and religious leaders – for example, by relating mass consumption of their product to social improvement. But social and political leaders no longer provide dramatic social visions for free. As a result, the supply of vision has to be 'privatized'; founders and chief executives have to provide their own visions to boost their firms' performance.

A focus on the firm itself, rather than the global system of which it forms a part, is certainly characteristic of much IB research. Many papers in the *Journal of International Business Studies* are concerned with the firm – in particular, with the organizational structure and corporate culture of the multinational enterprise – whilst relatively few analyse the IB system as a whole. Recent emphasis on resource-based theories of the firm has reinforced this narrow focus. Whereas in the 1960s IB theory was concerned mainly with the system, and the firm was largely ignored, today the 'pendulum' has swung to the opposite extreme, and research seems exclusively preoccupied with the firm rather than the system.

It is much easier to be dogmatic about a relatively simple subject like the firm than it is about a more complex subject such as the system as a whole; as noted earlier, dogmatization thrives on selecting partial aspects of a vision which are relatively easy to formalize. It is interesting to note that most of the dogmas in IB focus on the firm, whereas most of the visions focus on the system as a whole.

Public opinion is becoming increasingly concerned about the future of the system as a whole. This is partly in response to climate change, environmental degradation and terrorists threats, but the marketing and human resources strategies of Western multinationals have become targets of increasing criticism too. Many influential NGOs now pursue an explicit 'anti-globalization' agenda. The nature of the system as a whole is once again a matter of public debate. Thirty years ago the political debate over 'sovereignty at bay' stimulated the development and refinement of significant visions (Vernon, 1971). Similarly, the public today demands informed opinion on the IB system, but now most IB professionals are locked into a narrow preoccupation with the firm.

To express this point in 'dogmatic' terms, what is needed is less concern with the firm in isolation, and more concern with its 'environment'. Greater attention to the interaction of the firm with its environment would be an important step in the right direction. Ultimately, however, there is no substitute for 'going the whole way' and recovering those inspiring visions of the system as a whole.

Conclusion

Vision is an important element in the development of any theory. It is particularly important in the social sciences because the systems studied are so complex that formalization is difficult. Formalization is important in assuring the internal logical consistency of a theory.

But formalization almost always depends on some restrictive assumptions, made purely for analytical convenience, which partially distort, and thereby diminish, the impact of the vision. For this reason most dynamic areas of research are characterized by the coexistence of theory and vision. The theory sets out what can be achieved by formal modelling, given the limitations of current techniques, whilst vision points the way forward to a better theory that remains to be developed. This vision of a better theory inspires the research agenda in the subject.

IB is a highly complex subject. This means that it is not only resistant to formalization, but also that no single vision can really do justice to it. IB needs to draw upon several distinctive visions, and it is extremely fortunate that a suitable range of visions exists. These visions are based on different views of the degree of rationality in decision-making, the way that selection mechanisms (notably competition) operate, and how far deviations from equilibrium can persist. Because of these differences, the views are not simply different aspects of a single encompassing vision. Nevertheless, the visions complement each other. Some focus on explaining the location of activities, whilst others focus on institutional arrangements; some focus on tangible factors, such as population and natural resources, whilst others focus on intangible factors such as technology and culture.

Formalization has made limited progress in IB. Most formal models of IB are found in specialist economics journals, or in the fields of geography and operations research (where the logistics of IB activity are addressed). A few IB scholars have specified formal models but, by and large, the few models that have been formulated have not been taken up by the profession as a whole.

Formalization has proceeded instead through a growing recourse to dogma. In the context of IB, dogma may be regarded as a form of premature formalization, where apparently definitive statements are made about issues whose logic has not been fully worked out. Some dogmas have originated within IB, while others have been imported into it. The increasing use of Porter's 'five forces' in IB texts is a good example of imported dogma. This particular case is very unfortunate because, unlike the other areas of IB where dogma dominates, there are perfectly adequate formal models that describe how the five forces work.

Lack of vision is not unique to IB. In many disciplines the process of professionalization has resulted in loss of vision. In some cases vision has been replaced by formal theory, whereas in others, like IB, it has simply been replaced by dogma instead. Management studies has been particularly prone to this problem. The demand for dogma from busy executives, and the consultants who advise them, has distorted research incentives. Research focus has shifted from the IB system as a whole to the individual firm. It is ironic that at a time when the role of entrepreneurial vision in the growth of the firm has been strongly emphasized, the role of vision in the analysis of the IB system has declined. There has been too much emphasis on the firm as an isolated entity, and too little on the firm's environment.

Incentives are changing, however. There is a growing public demand for informed opinion on issues of global political economy, and a dearth of IB scholars with the breadth of vision to supply it. Somewhat perversely, it seems to be the older scholars, who are acquainted with the early visions, who are in the best position to meet this need, rather than the younger scholars, whose IB education excluded visionary elements. To create a new generation of IB scholars with the requisite vision, some radical changes are required in the profession. Greater opportunities need to be provided for the publication of visionary work, and young scholars need to be given more time to absorb and reflect on the visionary heritage of their subject.

References

Berlin, Isaiah (1953) *The Hedgehog and the Fox: an Essay on Tolstoy's View of History*. London: Weidenfeld & Nicolson.

Buchanan, James (1979) *What Should Economists Do?* Indianapolis, Indiana: Liberty Press.

Cantwell, John A. and Simona Iammarino (2003) *Multinational Corporations and European Regional Systems of Innovation*. London: Routledge.

Casson, Mark (1997) *Information and Organization: a New Perspective on the Theory of the Firm*. Oxford: Oxford University Press.

Casson, Mark and associates (1986) *Multinationals and World Trade: Vertical Integration and the Division of Labour in World Industries*. London: Allen & Unwin.

Coase, Ronald (1937) 'The Nature of the Firm', *Economica* (New series), 4: 386–405.

Debreu, Gerard (1959) *The Theory of Value: an Axiomatic Analysis of Economic Equilibrium*. New York: John Wiley.

Dicken, Peter (1998) *Global Shift: Industrial Change in a Turbulent World.* London: Harper & Row.

Dunning, John H. (1977) 'Trade, Location of Economic Activity and the Multinational Enterprise: a Search for an Eclectic Approach', in B.Ohlin, P-O. Hesselborn and P. M.Wijkman (eds) *The International Allocation of Economic Activity*, London: Macmillan – now Palgrave Macmillan.

Hannan, Michael T. and John Freeman (1989) *Organizational Ecology.* Cambridge, Mass.: Harvard University Press.

Hayek, Friedrich A. (1937) 'Economics and Knowledge', *Economica* (New series), 4: 33–54.

Hayek, Friedrich A. (1978) *New Studies in Philosophy, Politics, Economics and the History of Ideas.* London: Routledge and Kegan Paul.

Hennart, Jean-Francois (1982) *A Theory of Multinational Enterprise.* Ann Arbor: University of Michigan Press.

Hymer, Stephen H. (1976) *The International Operations of National Firms: a Study of Direct Investment.* Cambridge, Mass.: MIT Press.

McCann, Philip (1998) *Economics of Industrial Location: a Logistics Cost Approach.* Berlin: Springer.

Ricardo, David (1817) *Principles of Political Economy and Taxation* (ed. P. Sraffa), Cambridge: Cambridge University Press, 1951.

Robertson, Dennis H. (1923) *The Control of Industry.* London: Nisbet.

Samuelson, Paul (1948) 'International Trade and the Equalisation of Factor Prices', *Economic Journal*, 58: 163–84.

Schumpeter, Joseph A. (1934) *Theory of Economic Development* (ed. R. Opie), Cambridge, Mass.: Harvard University Press.

Schumpeter, Joseph A. (1939) *Business Cycles.* New York: McGraw-Hill.

Simon, Herbert A. (1957) 'A Formal Theory of the Employment Relation', in H. A. Simon, *Models of Man: Social and Rational*, New York: John Wiley.

Smith, Adam (1776) *An Inquiry into the Nature and Causes of the Wealth of Nations* (Glasgow edition). Oxford: Oxford University Press, 1976.

Vernon, Raymond (1971) *Sovereignty at Bay: the Multinational Spread of US Enterprises.* New York: Basic Books.

Williamson, Oliver E. (1975) *Markets and Hierarchies: Analysis and Anti-trust Implications.* New York: Free Press.

Williamson, Oliver E. (1985) *The Economic Institutions of Capitalism.* New York: Free Press.

3
Technological Determinism, Globalization and the Multinational Firm

Stephen J. Kobrin

> Men make their own history, but they do not make it just as they please; they do not make it under circumstances chosen by themselves, but under circumstances directly encountered and transmitted from the past.
>
> (Marx, 1869)

In *The Great Illusion*, Angell (1910) argued that national economies had become so complex and the international economy so integrated that war was now a logical absurdity: '... the world has passed out of that stage of development in which it is possible for one civilized group to advance its well-being by the military domination of another'. Less than a year after his last edition was published Europe plunged into the abyss of the Second World War.

It is difficult to determine when fundamental change has taken place in economics and politics. Angell assumed that the early twentieth century global world economy was a result of significant, qualitative changes in underlying material conditions; that both economic integration and the 'new' dominance of economics over politics were irreversible. He believed that the costs of war in terms of economic disruption had become unacceptable and the gains from military conquest so limited relative to those from trade and investment that armed attack was irrational. His belief in the rationality of decision makers was proven wrong quickly and tragically.

In *What Is History*, E. H. Carr (2001) asked 'How far are the facts of history facts about single individuals and how far social facts?' Isaiah Berlin paraphrased Marx in response to Carr's determinism:

'I see no reason for denying that men have a limited freedom of individual action, but within conditions that are largely not of their own choosing' (Evans, 2001, p. xxi). The question that both of them raise is to what extent 'social facts' or 'conditions' limit or constrain human choice; what are the relative explanatory power of material and ideational theories of political–economic change?

Economic globalization is not new. O'Rourke and Williamson (1999) divide the Atlantic economy into three distinct eras over the last 150 years: a *belle époque* of late nineteenth-century globalization, the dark middle ages of deglobalization from 1914 to 1950 and a renaissance of globalization in the late twentieth century. The late nineteenth and early twentieth centuries witnessed a 'high water mark' or 'golden age' of international economic integration; a relatively large number of authors have compared the current wave of globalization to the first, arguing that current levels of trade, capital flows and economic integration are far from unprecedented, that what we now are experiencing is but a 'second act' following the long intermission of the Great Depression, the Second World War and the Cold War.

The first wave of globalization came to a sudden end, crashing on the shoals of the Great Depression and/or imploding as a result of a popular backlash against the effects of free trade and large-scale immigration. The moral of the 'déjà vu all over again'[1] story is straightforward: globalization is neither inevitable nor irreversible and the second global age could end in much the same way as the first.

That argument rests on two assumptions, one or both of which have to be valid for it to hold. First, globalization could be a reflection of a particular, perhaps cyclical constellation of underlying economic and political conditions and its fragility would then result from change in those conditions. The simplest variant of that argument is that international economic liberalization is a luxury of 'good times', as national economic conditions deteriorate an open international economy becomes increasingly problematic. Second, globalization could be 'socially constructed', one choice among a relatively large number of modes of organization of the world economy which reflects the existing distribution of political power. As power shifts, perhaps as opposition to globalization grows among elites and/or the population at large, other choices are made.

Globalization redux

Lessons can be drawn from the economic history of the last century and a half to support opposing arguments about the sustainability of an open, liberal international economy. An economic optimist could see 'globalization' as the norm since the last third of the nineteenth century, interrupted only by the devastating events of what one hopes is an atypical century: the world wars, the Great Depression and the Cold War. On the other hand, a pessimist could just as easily argue that 'globalization' is the exception, occurring only when the world economy is dominated by a single hegemon, first Great Britain and then the United States.

In an article titled 'Is Globalization Reversible?', James (1999, p. 12) outlines the 'globalization as exceptionalism' argument:

> Analysts of globalization often present the process as irreversible – a one-way road to the future. But a more sober and pessimistic assessment would be more realistic. History is studded with examples of highly developed and integrated international communities that dissolved under the pressure of unexpected events.

While it is foolish to ignore the lessons of history it is reasonable to ask if they are still valid. The question, as always, is how to apply the past to the future.

The collapse of international trade and investment accompanied by competitive devaluations and inconvertibility during the Great Depression of the 1930s provide one obvious model. The Hawley–Smoot tariff of 1930 contained provisions for duties on 21,000 different goods which averaged well over 50 per cent. As virtually every nation tried to wall itself off from industrial collapse and unemployment, world exports (the absolute value, not the rate of growth) fell by two-thirds from January of 1930 to January 1933 (Kindleberger, 1986).

Protectionism and economic nationalism quickly replaced an open international economy as country after country retreated into autarky. As James (1999) notes, everything – labour, goods and capital – was now to be national; even Keynes argued for 'homespun goods' and national finance. In short, the end of the first global era was marked by walled-off, inward-looking national economies which prolonged and deepened the Great Depression.

A related argument ties globalization to economic cycles: expansions and contractions of financial liquidity and international investment. Booms are always followed by busts, and '(I)f liquidity expansions have pushed global integration forward, subsequent liquidity contractions have brought globalization to an unexpected halt' (Pettis, 2001).

In contrast, O'Rourke and Williamson (1999, p. 287) argue that war and depression were relevant but non-critical factors in the collapse of the first wave of globalization. They believe that globalization imploded as a result of a widespread political backlash to its actual or perceived distributional effects. 'Far from being destroyed by unforeseen and exogenous political events, globalization, at least in part, destroyed itself.' They argue that the backlash reflected the perceived effects of trade on incomes and land rents, and perhaps more important, the reaction to the massive flows of immigration that characterized the early twentieth century.

The first years of the twenty-first century certainly have a 'déjà vu all over again' feeling to them. The bursting of the 1990s stock market bubble and ensuing widespread economic difficulties have been associated with a sharp fall-off in flows of direct investment and a marked slowing of the rate of growth of world trade. Perhaps more important, there has been an increase in trade-related conflicts and protectionist measures including restrictions on imports of steel by the USA and major US–EU disputes over genetically modified organisms and other issues. As of mid-2004, the newest round of trade talks under the auspices of the World Trade Organization (the Doha round) appear mired in virtually intractable North–South conflict over intellectual property, investment rules and agricultural protectionism.

If economic crises were not enough, the events of 9/11 and the resulting 'war against terrorism' have been seen by many as the final straw that broke the camel's back. A watershed event marking a retreat behind national borders, a reassertion of the power of the nation-state, the re-emergence of 'high politics' – military and security issues – as a dominant force in world politics and a corresponding acceleration of the decline of the global world order. The chief economist of Morgan Stanley, for example, argued that the increased costs of international production and trade may result in 'the world turning its back on globalization', that the terrorist attacks and their aftermath 'may bring about its demise' (Roach, 2001).

Last, virtually every international meeting since the ill-fated Seattle trade negotiations in the fall of 1999 has been accompanied by large, loud and sometimes violent anti-globalization protests. While the protest movement can be chaotic, less than articulate and uncertain about alternative futures, it should not be dismissed. It may reflect widespread angst and anxiety about the direction that globalization has taken, a sense of loss of control over democratic outcomes and a lack of faith in the legitimacy of international institutions.

While much of the concern about globalization (and free flows of trade and investment, in general) reflects immediate economic insecurity, the protest movement is also motivated by what Berry (1999) calls *post-material* interests such as human rights, cultural homogenization (McDonaldization) and the environment. Furthermore, many of the anti-globalization protesters assume that the reversal of globalization is a matter of political will. That 'Globalization . . . involves a conscious process of restructuring and reconstituting the global political economy – molding international, regional, national, and local institutions to serve the increasing economic integration of the world' (Lichbach and Almeida, 2001, p. 5). There is an assumption that globalization is corporate globalization, a mode of political–economic organization that reflects and privileges the power of multinational corporations in world and national politics.

'What is history?', our answer, consciously or unconsciously, reflects our own position in time, and forms part of our answer to the broader question what view we take of the society in which we live' (Carr, 2001, p. 2). The first era of globalization, the *belle époque*, did come to an end: the world economy slammed shut in 1930 and it did not begin to open up again until well after the Second World War. The historical fact of 'the end of globalization' certainly legitimizes asking whether the current wave of globalization is reversible.

Determining whether some combination of economic or political dislocation and/or popular opposition will result in the end of the second global era, however, depends on whether or not – or perhaps to what degree – we judge the lessons of history applicable. Have the material conditions underlying globalization changed fundamentally in the last 70-odd years and, if so, do those changes limit or constrain our choice of modes of organization of the world economy?

I will argue that the answer to that question is yes. Technological change has altered significantly the costs of alternative modes of organization of the world economy to the point where our range of choice is limited. To be clear, that *does not* mean that social, economic or political structures are rigidly determined by technology or that it is impossible for policy makers to make 'irrational' choices. Pursuing that argument requires an exploration of the intellectually dangerous topic of technological determinism. It is to that subject I now turn.

Technological determinism

What is the relationship between technology, or material factors more generally, and changes in social, political and economic organization: as Heilbroner (1994, p. 54) famously put it, 'Do machines make history?' His answer is necessarily complex and indeterminate.

> That machines make history in some sense – that the level of technology has a direct bearing on the human drama – is of course obvious. That they do not make all of history, however … is equally clear. The challenge, then, is to see whether one can order the problem so that it becomes intellectually manageable.

Marx drew a direct link between cause and effect. The often quoted sentences from the Preface to the *Critique of Political Economy* speak for themselves:

> In the social production of their existence, men inevitably enter into definite relations, which are *independent of their will*, namely relations of production appropriate to a given stage in the development of their material forces of production. The totality of these relations of production constitutes the economic structure of society, the real foundation, on which arises a legal and political superstructure. (Marx, 1859, pp. 20–1, emphasis added)

Historical materialism is generally seen as hard technological determinism in which steadily growing, autonomous, technological development determines the course of events. Marx argued that 'history is, fundamentally, the growth of human productive power, and forms of society rise and fall according as they enable or impede that growth' (Cohen, 2000, p. x). Hard determinism assumes that technology is a force outside of direct human control, that it has a tendency to grow over time, and that it is material conditions rather than ideas that determine that nature of the socio-economic order: 'It is not the consciousness of men that determines their existence, but their social existence that determines their consciousness' (Marx, 1859, p. 21). In Bimber's (1994, p. 84) terms, 'nomological' determinism assumes that technological developments are not socially or culturally determined and that these processes, once begun, force social adaptation and change.[2]

At this point, few observers would argue for 'hard' determinism, that 'machines make history' in a direct causal sense. Once one moves away from hard determinism, however, what is left of technological determinism, of a cause and effect relationship between changes in the material base and the political–economic order?

In answering that question, Heilbroner (1994, p. 62) is careful not to throw the baby out with the bathwater:

> ... to relegate technology from an undeserved position of *primum mobile* in history to that of a mediating factor, both acted upon by, and acting upon the body of society, is not to write off its influence but only to specify its mode of operation with greater precision.

'Soft' versions of technological determinism envision a more nuanced and complex relationship between technology and the social order. Technology is not an autonomous, self-propelled force. It is embedded in the social order and the relationship between the material base and the larger society is reciprocal: technology both drives change and 'responds discriminatingly to social pressures' (Smith, 1994, p. 2). Technology and technological progress are social activities, responsive to social direction.

Furthermore, while technology may drive change, its impact is both limited and contingent. As Skolnikoff (1993, p. 10) notes, science and technology can result in change in the international political system, but these changes do not result simply because of the existence of new scientific knowledge, but through '... the actions of actors in the political and economic system, through the choices they make, through the cumulative responses of society'.

In contrast, Wendt (1999) argues that a basic tenet of idealism is that shared ideas rather than material forces determine the structures of human association, that it is 'ideas all the way down'. He suggests that the relationship between materialism and idealism is bipolar rather than continuous, that materialists who argue that 'brute' material forces drive social forms cluster at one end of a continuum and idealists who believe that the deep structure of society is determined by ideas at the other. Keohane (2000, p. 126) responded that

> The social world is not one of either/or. We are all aware of the mixture of material factors and ideas that affects our everyday lives; so it is not immediately clear why we should have to choose between materialism and idealism.... We cannot imagine society – and we certainly could not explain social relationships – without reference to both material forces and human consciousness.

Leaving aside the question of what is meant by material conditions or technology for the moment, the challenge is to thread a reasonable course between the poles of hard materialism where it is technology rather than ideas that determine social structures and an idealism where 'consciousness' determines 'social existence', where the social order – and more specifically international political and economic organization – is built entirely on a foundation of ideas and social action.

I would certainly agree that science and technology have become the 'most powerful and persistent factors leading to social change and ... to change in international affairs' (Skolnikoff, 1993, p. 3). The fundamental structures of globalization, deep integration and networked interconnectedness, are a result of significant technological changes such as the digital and information revolutions and the dramatically increased scale and speed of technological innovation itself. However, that is not to say that globalization, as a specific mode of political–economic organization, is rigidly determined by technological change.

Whether an alternative is feasible or plausible is a function of its social and economic cost. While autarky is possible – North Korea provides an example – I argue that its cost would not be seen as acceptable in most societies in the world today. In fact, I will argue that technological change limits the range of alternatives to those consistent with a *relatively* open and integrated global world economy, that the costs of closure in all but the most exceptional circumstances are no longer acceptable.

The problem, of course, is that we have been here before. Any number of books and articles written before the First World War argued that the first wave of globalization was a function of technological change, that the global world economy resulted directly from the nineteenth-century revolutions in transport and communications: railroads; steamships; the telegraph; and telephone (Baldwin and Martin, 1999). Angell was not alone: other authors argued that the technology had changed the world irreversibly, that a retreat from an integrated global economy was no longer possible. What is different this time around?

Globalization and technological change

Discussing global finance, Cohen (1996, p. 4) summarizes for possible models or hypotheses explaining globalization. The first, a liberal model, emphasizes the impacts of competition and innovation in the marketplace, stressing 'advances in communications and information technologies, which have literally swept away institutional and legal barriers to market integration ...'. A second realist model emphasizes the role of policy rivalries among governments. The third focuses on domestic politics and the last, cognitive factors and belief systems.

While not discounting the applicability of all four models, I argue that changes in technology, the material base of globalization, produce effects which then serve to constrain, *but not determine*, political–economic organization. Technological change, primarily the digital and information revolutions, has 'swept away' barriers resulting in new, deep forms of networked integration which would be very costly to reverse both in terms of the difficulty of unravelling them and the efficiency loss in doing so.

The 1930s provide the model for the 'end of globalization', a return to severe limits on trade, investment and currency convertibility. While the events of the twentieth century certainly demonstrate that states are capable of virtually anything, I will argue that forecasts of the end of globalization must be framed in terms of its cost, and that the cost of a prolonged retreat behind national economic borders would be very difficult to sustain at this point. The costs of autarky would not be acceptable to the vast majority of citizens of democratic polities.

As noted above, the first wave of globalization was, to a large extent, a function of the nineteenth-century revolutions in communications and transport. Developments in communications had immediate impacts; for example, linking the United States and Europe though the first transatlantic telegraph cable in 1865 (Standage, 1998) resulted in a relatively rapid convergence of Treasury Bond prices in New York and London. However, developments in transport – railroads and steamships – were demonstrably more important the first time around. The marked improvements in transport facilitated marked increases in flows of goods across borders, the dramatic long-term increase in international trade, that characterized the first wave of globalization. (The developments of railroads and steamships also facilitated the sharp increases in flows of people, of international migration, in the late nineteenth and early twentieth century.)

The development of steamships in the mid-nineteenth century reduced the voyage across the Atlantic from months to less than two weeks almost instantly. More important, it provided reliability in terms of relatively fixed delivery schedules. International telegraph and telephone cables also provided dramatic changes, reducing communication times from that of human travel to the virtually instantaneous. That being said, the developments in transport and communication of the late twentieth century still represent a qualitative leap, a quantum jump if you will, from those just discussed.

As Baldwin and Martin note (1999, p. 1), the two waves of globalization are similar in that they were both driven by 'radical reductions in technical and policy barriers to international transactions'. They argue, however, that there is a fundamental difference: the importance of trade in *goods* the first time around versus trade in *ideas* the second.

In the last two decades of the twentieth century the world was integrated through reliable and relatively cheap real-time communications networks: international telephony; cellphones; fax; and most important, the development and rapid expansion of satellite communications and the Internet. The cost of three-minute phone call from New York to London, for example, fell from around $250 in the 1930s to well under a dollar by the end of the century; the average price per minute for an international call was estimated at $0.25 in the late 1990s (Cairncross, 1997). The worldwide Internet population was estimated at 580–655 million in 2002 and is forecast to grow rapidly to 709–945 million by 2004 (Cyber Atlas Staff, 2003).[3]

The development of long-range, wide-bodied jet aircraft during the second half of the twentieth century also represents a qualitative change. To note that being able to get anywhere in the world in a day markedly facilitates the shipment of goods – at least those with a high value to weight ratio – is to state the obvious. Perhaps more important, however, is the ability of people – of managers, scientists, engineers and regulators – to cross large distances quickly, easily and relatively cheaply. By the 1990s, flying across the Atlantic for a one-day meeting was not unusual. Jet transport allows for direct, interpersonal communication across relatively large distances, interpersonal communication that facilitates the exchange of ideas.

Two other technological developments are of direct interest. First, the tendency of atoms to morph into bits (Negroponte, 1995), for hard goods such as compact discs, books and artwork to take the form of electrons which can be easily replicated and transmitted from any computer on the Net to any other computer on the Net. Second is the dramatic increase in the cost, risk and complexity of the development of technology. US corporate R&D spending, for example, increased over eightfold (in constant dollars) from 1960 to 2000 (National Science Foundation, 2000).

The impact of technology

These dramatic changes in technology result in a form of globalization that is qualitatively different from the first wave, it is deeper, networked rather than hierarchical and encompasses the social, cultural and political spheres as well as the economic. I will discuss five aspects of the global world economy as examples:

- The internationalization of production
- Efficiency-driven FDI
- Internationalization of services
- Internationalization of R&D
- NGOs as a manifestation of globalization

The dramatic drop in transport cost during the nineteenth century led to a sharp increase in international trade; indeed Baldwin and Martin (1999, p. 11) argue that 'large-scale international trade was born in the nineteenth century'. Total trade as a proportion of GDP was remarkably high for many of the developed countries in 1910, then fell markedly in the 1930s and the pre-First World War levels were not achieved again in most countries until the 1980s. Similarly, given the very high level of capital flows, the late nineteenth and early twentieth century has been called the golden age of international economic integration.

If one simply looks at the numbers, the relative importance of trade and capital flows, the second wave of globalization does not seem to be remarkable. The ratio of trade to GDP, for example, was 44 per cent in 1910 versus 57 per cent in 1995 for the UK, 38 per cent versus 46 per cent for Germany, 35 per cent versus 43 per cent for France and 11 per cent versus 24 per cent for the USA. In some countries the importance of capital flows has actually declined. Current account as a per cent of GDP was 4.6 for the UK in the 1890–1913 period versus 2.6 in 1989–96, 1.3 versus 0.7 for France, 1.0 versus 1.2 for the USA and 1.5 versus 2.7 for Germany (Baldwin and Martin, 1999, pp. 8 and 15).

The quality of those flows, however, is dramatically different. Before the First World War trade flows consisted of arm's length shipments of raw materials and manufactured goods. Most of the capital flows were portfolio investment rather than direct investment supporting trade or production (Bordo *et al.*, 1999). International integration was broad but not particularly deep.

In contrast, globalization now entails the internationalization of production itself. Sixty-five thousand transnational corporations with 850,000 affiliates dominate the international economy. The affiliates of these firms account for 10 per cent of world GDP, one-third of world exports and, perhaps more important, the value of the sales of these affiliates is over twice that of world exports (United Nations Conference on Trade and Development, 2002). Moreover, while estimates are difficult to come by, it appears that between 30 and 50 per cent of world 'trade' is actually comprised of intra-firm transfers between units of multinational firms; for example a recent study of US trade patterns found that 38 per cent of transactions were intra-firm (Clausing, 2001).

A second important and closely related change is a shift from traditional market-oriented or resource-seeking investment to efficiency-seeking FDI; multinational firms splitting up and internationalizing the value chain of production. This entails very complex international integration strategies with firms combining their own mobile resources with immobile country-based resources (Dunning, 2002).

> What is distinct about the rise of international production systems as opposed to earlier TNC operations is, first, the intensity of integration both on a regional and global scale, and second, the emphasis on the efficiency of the system as a whole. Global markets therefore increasingly involve competition between entire production systems orchestrated by TNCs, rather than between individual factories or firms. (United Nations Conference on Trade and Development, 2002, p. xxi)

Systems of international production involve complex networks of firms integrated through both direct investment and a wide range of alliances and contractual arrangements. Firms locate various components of their production and service functions worldwide to take advantage of differences in costs, resources, logistics and markets (United Nations Conference on Trade and Development, 2002). The internationalization of production depends on global, real-time communications and information systems that allow for centralized control of the very complex networks of investment and outsourced contractual relations. It is a function of the 'trade in ideas', of complex, real-time cross-border transfers of technology and management.

The closure of the international economy in the 1930s was accomplished relatively easily through high tariff walls and limits on investment. In many instances domestic or 'homespun' goods could be substituted for imports. While the costs were considerable in terms of deepening and prolonging the Great Depression, they were still marginal and incremental.

At this point, unravelling the very complex networks of international production systems would be considerably more difficult and more costly. Closing national borders would require recreating complex, internationalized systems of production domestically. As it is far from clear that individual firms, or even individual national economies, have that capability, attempts to radically restrict flows of goods, capital and technology would result in very severe and widespread dislocations. As noted above, I believe that the costs of closure would be too high to be acceptable.

While changes in technology underlying globalization have made complex international production networks possible, changes in the cost, risk and complexity of that technology have made it necessary in many industries. In sectors such as telecommunications, pharmaceuticals, aerospace, semiconductors and biotechnology the cost of a competitive research and development budget, relative to revenues, is so high as to require global markets.

US industrial R&D expenditures and R&D to sales ratios have risen consistently in recent decades, both reaching an all-time high in 2000 (the R&D to sales ratio averaged 3.6 per cent across all industries). Total American industrial R&D spending rose 13 per cent in 2000 to $180.4 billion (Wolfe, 2002).

The American pharmaceutical industry serves as an example. In 2002 pharmaceutical firms spent $32,051 million on R&D, 16.3 per cent of their global sales. If that level of R&D expenditures had to be supported on domestic sales alone, it would have accounted for 22 per cent of sales. In contrast, in 1970, pharmaceutical firms' R&D spending accounted for only 9.3 per cent of total sales or 13.6 per cent of domestic sales. International R&D accounted for 9 per cent of spending in 1970 and 21 per cent in 2002 (PhRMA, 2003).

The cost and risk of technological development have become so high that firms must market their goods in a large number of countries if outlays are to be recovered, in that sense markets are inherently global. Furthermore, the complexity of technological development combined with the pressure for rapid innovation requires the internationalization of research. The response to the recent SARS threat, which involved simultaneous research in laboratories in a number of different countries linked via digital communications, provides an example.

Technology both enables and, at least to some degree, requires, globalization. It far from clear that the costs of unravelling networks and withdrawing from international markets in terms of a slower rate of innovation for an AIDS vaccine or effective cancer treatment would be acceptable. Even if it were possible to develop a new AIDS vaccine in a single market, would German consumers, for example, consider it reasonable to wait for a 'homespun' version?

A fourth example of the impact of technological change on the nature of international integration is provided by the trend towards the internationalization of services. Digitalization combined with

Internet or satellite communications allows for spatial disbursal of the value chain for services as well as manufacturing. Exports of the Indian software industry, for instance, grew at an *annual* rate of 43 per cent from 1991/92 to 2001/02 with a total volume of $7800 million estimated for 2002/03 (Heeks, 2003). A relatively large proportion of Indian software exports are services rather than products; Indian software providers are linked via the Internet or satellite to computers in New York or London. Indian firms are responsible for maintenance upgrades and installing new software on computers halfway around the world.

Similarly, the outsourcing of other services such as call centers, tax preparation and even financial analysis to countries where an educated and capable labour force is available at prices well below those in the USA or Europe is growing rapidly. The internationalization of services is made possible by both digitalization and the global communications system. It results in a deep, complex and networked pattern of international integration that would be difficult to unravel. Again, the issue is the cost and the feasibility of substituting domestic for foreign resources.

Last, globalization now extends well beyond the world economy to networks of relationships among large numbers of heterogeneous social, cultural and political, as well as economic organizations. The current world order has been characterized as a 'place inhabited by de-territorialized communities, fragmented identities, transnational corporations and cyber spatial flows of finance' (Deibert, 1997, p. ix).

A sign held by protesters at a recent meeting of the World Economic Forum in Davos read 'Our Opposition is as Global as Your Oppression'. Trade in ideas is not limited to the multinational firm, large numbers of advocacy groups and non-governmental organizations are global in scope with diverse local entities linked directly by the Internet, though websites and e-mail.

Materialism and social choice

We are left with questions, first about the relative power of material and ideational explanations of globalization and then the extent to which material conditions actually constrain human choice. In arguing for material limits on human choice, Marx notes that 'The tradition of all the dead generations weighs like a nightmare on the brain of the living' (Marx, 1869, p. 15). The recurring 'nightmare' in this context is that we have been there before, arguments about techno-logical change and irreversibility are not new. As noted above, the first wave of globalization was explained in terms of revolutionary technological developments in transport and communications; predictions of its immortality, however, proved short-lived.

Much of the discussion of globalization confuses its particular con-figuration at any point in time (outcome) with process or its underlying structure (Hargittai and Centeno, 2001). There is no question that the underlying structure of late twentieth century globalization – deep integration and complex networked interconnectedness – is materially determined; it is a function of revolutionary developments in transport and particularly digital communications technology that sustain complex networks. I suspect that even those who argue that a global world economy reflects and privileges existing constellations of power, would agree that it would not be possible without the digital and information revolutions.

The way the global economy is configured at any given point is, to some extent, socially constructed. Thus, some of the more controversial aspects of globalization such as the spread of American consumer culture ('McDonaldization'), the emphasis on complete deregulation and the 'Washington Consensus', and patterns of poverty and inequality reflect one particular configuration of the global economy among a number of possible choices.

That being said, I would argue that technological change has rendered the basic process of globalization, deep integration and networked interconnectedness, irreversible. At the risk of oversimpli-fication, possible modes of organization of the world economy can be seen as lying on a continuum ranging from relatively complete autarky on the one hand to relatively complete openness on the other. The 'end of globalization' in terms of closure, severe limits on flows of goods, capital, technology and perhaps even people, is no longer possible. As discussed above, the cost of reverting to relatively autonomous national economies would not be acceptable.

The question is where one draws the line. First, I have discussed only two points on the continuum: a relatively open international economy and a retreat to autarky. There are a large number of points in between and it is certainly possible to envision national policy makers acting 'to moderate the degree of globalization without throwing the baby out with the bath water'.[4] Furthermore, attempts by policy makers to close their borders in the short term are not inconceivable.

Second, the impact of technological change may vary across functional components of globalization. Thus, Garrett (2000, p. 976) argues that while technological determinism provides a 'parsimonious explanation' for the integration of financial markets, it is much less effective as an explanation of flows of trade or FDI.

Furthermore, arguing that the acceptable range of modes of organization of the world economy is contingent on technology *is not* to argue that the Washington Consensus is technologically determined, that is the only possible outcome. Some constraints on flows of goods, capital and technology certainly are feasible. However, a reversion back to anything even approaching the closures of the 1930s is not. Technological change has limited the applicability of the lessons of history in this instance. A *relatively* open, networked world economy, and indeed, transnational social, cultural and political networks, are here to stay.

That is not necessarily good news. Dysfunctional globalization, an integrated world economy which neither works well nor allows for an escape behind national borders, is certainly possible. One can imagine globalization characterized by increasing disputes among states and increasing opposition from large segments of the population, with only limited alternatives available in terms of other modes of economic organization. Avoiding dysfunctional globalization will require a world economy that is both more equitable (in terms of distribution), more pluralistic (in terms of organization of its component national units) and some form of global governance: international economic institutions which are both effective and legitimate.

Acknowledgement

I would like to thank Benjamin J. Cohen for his comments on an earlier version.

Notes

1. Attributed to Yogi Berra, wordsmith and N. Y. Yankees catcher.
2. Bimber argues that Marx was not a 'hard' determinist, but rather sees technology as more of an enabling factor than an autonomous force.

3. It should be noted that development of the 'global' communications network is very uneven, at this point about half of the world's population have never made a telephone call.
4. Communication from Benjamin Cohen, August 2003.

References

Angell, Norman (1910) *The Great Illusion: a Study of the Relation of Military Power in Nations to their Economic and Social Advantage*. New York and London: G. P. Putnam's Sons.

Baldwin, Richard E. and Philippe Martin (1999) *Two Waves of Globalization: Superficial Similarities, Fundamental Differences*. Cambridge: National Bureau of Economic Research.

Berry, Jeffrey M. (1999) *The New Liberalism: the Rising Power of Citizen Groups*. Washington, DC: The Brookings Institution.

Bimber, Bruce (1994) 'Three Faces of Technological Determinism', in Merritt Roe Smith and Leo Marx (eds) *Does Technology Drive History*. Cambridge: MIT Press.

Bordo, Michael, Barry Eichengreen and Douglas Irwin (1999) *Is Globalization Really Different Today Than Globalization a Hundred Years Ago?* Cambridge: National Bureau of Economic Research.

Cairncross, Frances (1997) *The Death of Distance*. Boston: Harvard Business School Press.

Carr, E. H. (2001) *What Is History?* Houndmills, Basingstroke, Hampshire: Palgrave.

Clausing, Kimberly (2001) *The Behavior of Intrafirm Trade Prices in U.S. International Price Data*. Washington: Bureau of Labor Statistics.

Cohen, Benjamin J. (1996) 'Phoenix Risen: the Resurrection of Global Finance' *World Politics*, 48(2): 268–96.

Cohen, G. A. (2000) *Karl Marx's Theory of History: a Defence* (expanded edition). Princeton: Princeton University Press.

Cyber Atlas Staff (2003) *Population Explosion*: Cyber Atlas.

Deibert, Ronald J. (1997) *Parchment, Printing, and Hypermedia: Communication in World Order Transformation*. New York: Columbia University Press.

Dunning, John H. (2002) *Global Capitalism, FDI and Competitiveness*: Vol. II: *The Selected Essays of John H. Dunning*. Northampton: Edward Elgar Publishing.

Evans, Richard J. (2001) 'Introduction', in E. H. Carr (ed.) *What Is History?* Houndmills, Basingstroke, Hampshire: Palgrave.

Garrett, Geoffrey (2000) 'The Causes of Globalization', *Comparative Political Studies*, 33(6–7): 941–91.

Hargittai, Eszter and Miguel Angel Centeno (2001) 'Defining a Global Geography', *American Behavioral Scientist*, 44(10): 1545–60.

Heeks, Richard (2003) Indian software export figures.

Heilbroner, Robert L. (1994) 'Do Machines Make History?' in Merritt Roe Smith and Leo Marx (eds) *Does Technology Drive History: the Dilemma of Technological Determinism*. Cambridge: MIT Press.

James, Harold (1999) 'Is Liberalization Reversible?' *Finance and Development*, December: 11–14.

Keohane, Robert O. (2000) 'Ideas Part-way Down', *Review of International Studies*, 26: 125–30.

Kindleberger, Charles P. (1986) *The World in Depression, 1929–39*. Berkeley: The University of California Press.

Lichbach, Mark I. and Paul Almeida (2001) *Global Order and Local Resistance: the Neoliberal Institutional Trilemma and the Battle of Seattle*. Riverside: Department of Sociology, University of California-Riverside.

Marx, Karl (1859) *A Contribution to the Critique of Political Economy*. New York: International Publishers, 1970.

Marx, Karl (1869) *The Eighteenth Brumaire of Louis Bonaparte*. New York: International Publications, Inc., 1975.

National Science Foundation (2000) *Research and Development in Industry*. National Science Foundation.

Negroponte, Nicholas (1995) *Being Digital*. New York: Knopf.

O'Rourke, Kevin H. and Jeffrey G. Williamson (1999) *Globalization and History: the Evolution of a Nineteenth-century Atlantic Economy*. Cambridge, Mass.: MIT Press.

Pettis, Michael (2001) 'Will Globalization Go Bankrupt', *Foreign Policy*, 126 (September–October).

PhRMA (2003) *Industry Profile 2003*. Pharmaceutical Research Manufacturers of America.

Roach, Stephen (2001) 'Back to Border', *Financial Times*. London.

Skolnikoff, Eugene (1993) *The Elusive Transformation: Science, Technology and the Evolution of International Politics*. Princeton: Princeton University Press.

Smith, Merrit Roe (1994) 'Technological Determinism in American Culture', in Merritt Roe Smith and Leo Marx (eds) *Does Technology Drive History: the Dilemma of Technological Determinism*. Cambridge: MIT Press.

Standage, Tom (1998) *The Victorian Internet*. New York: Walker and Company.

United Nations Conference on Trade and Development (2002) *World Investment Report 2002*. New York and Geneva: United Nations.

Wendt, Alexander (1999) *Social Theory of International Politics*. Cambridge, New York: Cambridge University Press.

Wolfe, Raymond (2002) *InfoBrief*. Sciences Resources Statistics.

4

Of Beauty Finding the Relevant Beast: the Field of International Business and the Dialogue of Fact and Theory

Bruce Kogut

Peter Buckley's request to write a short essay on what is international business prevailed over my usual reluctance to engage such questions because he alluded to the analogy of Edward Carr's *What Is History?* Why would I be reluctant and why would the reference to Carr persuade me?

My reluctance reflects simply two intuitions. The first is that it is more interesting to allocate one's time to doing what international business is than prescribing what it should be. Jacob Viner defined economics as 'what economists do'. Though this comment was made no doubt with a whimsical flourish, it is an excellent sociological definition. Communities are self-referential, they establish their truths by preferred styles, and they gravitate to new problems on the basis of the past achievements that they value. The best guide for future research is to contribute directly to that future. How feeble is the convention to end an article by indicating future research – which is usually no more than a statement of an author's current research!

The second intuition is the early experience in my career that such discussions reflect a call to abandon ship. Academic communities are viable as long as they provide career paths for new entrants. As much as ideas count, the world is not always just and hence the easy translation of important ideas to employment cannot be assumed. A viable community of research must create evident pathways of success. These pathways include journals to publish research, Ph.D.

programmes to educate candidates, and positions for graduates to populate. Together these two intuitions constitute a belief in the sociology of knowledge as based on practitioner communities and in the economics of careers based on incentives and rewards.

The element of careers in academic choice is not to be dismissed as the petty side of the business. James March has argued in various writings that smart people choose fields in which their smartness can be unambiguously ranked. Since the hard sciences are less ambiguous than the social sciences, March claimed, the average intelligence is likely to be higher in these fields. However, this reasoning has an element of deceitful play. For given that James March is a smart person and he chose social sciences, we have to conclude that either he is modest, he made an early career mistake, or he is wrong. Was Picasso lacking in intelligence when he chose painting, which surely is a field that has a large element of ambiguity in the codification of 'performance'? One may object and say that painting reflects a different competence than intelligence, though we should all quickly run for cover in trying to defend what exactly is then intelligence.

However, this obsession with performance and intelligence to derive career choice deflects a more engaging observation. Academic communities evidence as well an aesthetic. One senses this aesthetic easily in reviewing the variety of research in economics, even within mathematical economics. Consider, for example, the academic articles of Robert Solow, who is a staunch defender of the use of mathematics. These articles consist of formal models, but are generally absent of any proofs. Mathematics to Solow may be a type of filter: if you want to play the game, then you need to demonstrate mathematical competence. And it may also be a commitment to the demonstration of logic. For if we can't say it formally, then we don't know it in the first place.

Solow's implicit positioning is not much different than John Maynard Keynes, who first made his reputation in subjective probability theory. Keynes used mathematics less than contemporary economists, but he nevertheless put a value on its utility. In his *Principles of Economics*, Marshall relegated the mathematics to an appendix; still, the mathematics was included.

Compare these approaches to many economic articles that consist of a series of theorems, lemmas and proofs. This type of research is significant in trying to establish results under the most general conditions. In fact, whereas many were content to have established results under the calculus of variations, current economics seeks to provide proofs using newer mathematics, for example, topology, that is more general and less restrictive in the assumptions regarding continuity and smoothness. The appeal of this endeavour might be to raise the hurdle and hence render the criteria of ranking more transparent. Or it may well be that it reflects a particular aesthetic. To paraphrase Keats, formal is beauty, and beauty, formal. The cost of this aesthetic, however, may well be a sacrifice of 'other' economics than current economics. After all, human resources are scarce and their allocation implies a trade-off.

It is instructive to consider mathematics in physics. In his book *Rules and Representation*, Noam Chomsky mused that it might be the case that the mathematics that our brains are capable of producing correspond by chance to the 'true' mathematics that governs the primal forces of the universe, but it would be, one might add, an amazing coincidence. The case for the use of mathematics is surely compelling: the complexity of the phenomena and the enormity of data require non-linguistic languages by which to analyse the deeper structures and emergent properties. And yet it is rarer to see theorem and proofs as the dominant style of physics than economics.[1]

These comparisons suggest that the style of research in a community is more than just an outcome of optimization in finding the best methods and mode of inquiry. The style reflects as well a shared aesthetic. At the same time – and here is the critical observation – this aesthetic acts as an important filter for the selection and promotion of talent. In this sense, careers are not simply the desire of smart people looking to be unambiguously ranked, but also reflect a matching and learning process. A young person begins with an aptitude that reflects a conjoint of ability and preferences. This aptitude leads by a process of homophily to the seeking of 'like' others. The preferences are reciprocated, the engagement in producing products that reflect these preferences are rewarded, and hence a positive dynamic is created by which communities absorb new entrants and sustain themselves and their activities.

I am proposing, then, that an academic community is defined by a shared aesthetic that defines research styles as well as the dynamics of labour markets. However, as long as these communities are self-referential, the labour markets will not be a constraint on the evolution of this aesthetic as much as its expression. In short, the random drift in an academic, or any artistic, community will generate an internal dynamic than governs its intellectual evolution.

This proposition is, of course, the nightmare of the university president who responds to the hiring and funding demands of these communities by seeking resources from external constituents. This balancing act has often been seen as a dangerous trade-off. In the post-Second World War environment, there was an active debate over the imposition of US government funding that was too applied. The often secret nature of research due to national security led to the charge that open science was in danger of becoming closed science. Such dangers are currently often attributed to the encroachment of private enterprise funding.

The American university model is frequently internationally admired for its adaptive response to the opportunities presented by commercial funding. This funding has no doubt contributed to the ways that universities see the evolving division of labour of scientific work. Whereas the balance of academic independence and external demands is without question not an easy achievement, it is striking how the resolution consists not only of a trade-off, but of creative evolution. Thus, the sciences of physics, chemistry and biology have branched and recombined into numerous new fields that constitute 'disciplines'. An excellent example are the life sciences, which consist as much of chemistry and biology as of computer science and combinatorial mathematics. There has been a genesis of new fields in the sciences.

On the other hand, it is puzzling that the four 'disciplines' of the social sciences (i.e. economics, sociology, psychology and anthropology) emerged at the start of the last century and that since then, there has been no successful new discipline. Occasionally, a social science discipline announces itself interested in another area's domain. There has been a significant amount of economic imperialism – often labelled as such – that extends optimization or game theory to other social (and hard) sciences. Sociology has recently proposed a field of 'economic sociology'. Yet, neither economics nor sociology have a pronounced interest in the other's disciplinary domain that would constitute a new discipline. Both efforts represent extensions, not new combinations.

The puzzle is all the more salient in the context of the organization of graduate business schools. Business schools preserve by and large the social science disciplines, though there are particular unique specializations. A composite field such as strategy is an excellent example. Few, if any, schools have successfully been able to create an integrated disciplinary approach to the study of strategy. In schools such as Northwestern University, strategy qua economics is taught by a game theory department; strategy qua organizations is taught by an organizational behaviour group.

An area that might come closest to a new discipline is management. There is, in fact, a useful discourse among economists and organization theorists regarding the nature of the firm, its purpose and its strategy. However, this field has not emerged as a discipline despite large conferences that bear its name. I make this assertion based on a particular acid test. One who does economics is an economist; sociology is done by a sociologist. But one who does management is what? If the cost of Adam's eviction from the Garden of Eden was knowledge and the right to name and categorize knowledge, then it is odd that management lacks a nominative for those who pursue its study.

This same observation can be made for strategy. Organizational studies is slightly saved because its division into micro and macro has been denominated – by whatever logic is anyone's guess – as organizational behaviour and organizational theory. These labels lend themselves to behaviourists and theorists, both of which have legitimizing and aggrandizing connotations but are otherwise without much content in their opposition. Organizational sociology, or organizational economics, represents on the other hand plausible descriptions, because they preserve the disciplinary nominative, hence serving as a QED for my argument.

This conservatism is reflected in journal titles that rely upon 'science' for their legitimation. In part, this use of the word 'science' in the title reflects a period effect, as many management journals were founded subsequent to the blistering Ford Report in the 1950s on the lack of academic and scientific rigour in business education. However, even journals of recent founding, such as *Organization Science*, have relied upon this legitimation. The fancy clothing, I suspect, reflects a deep insecurity regarding the weather-readiness of the collective ship. What could be more damning to the 'science' of business than to appear as context sensitive. To many, context sensitivity is equivalent to the storytelling teaching of the pre-Ford Report era.

These observations lead us to the disheartening conclusion that a field that seeks to be integrative in the context of a business school is cursed with a pathological reaction motivated by discipline envy. The more applied is the institution, the more paranoid over its epistemological foundation appears to be the implication. No wonder, then, programmes of international business are often engaged in 'disciplinary' battles with business functions, such as finance, marketing or management. My informal empiricism tells me that international business as an area of study has been in a stable retreat in the United States (though expanding elsewhere), not because the phenomena under study have disappeared, but because the 'functional disciplines' – a delightful oxymoron – have viewed such pursuits somewhat along the lines of the Albigensian heresy.

This hostility is all the more curious in light of the treatment of the international domain in the conventional social science disciplines. International economics has a long line of Nobel-prize winning practitioners, political science accepts no less than two international domains (institutions and foreign policy), sociology has a proud history of comparative work, and anthropology has in its foundations been the study of comparative cultures. Why do these disciplines accept international studies as a domain whereas (American) business schools contest this legitimation?

In large part, this hostility is the echo of the harrowing experience of the Ford reports that gave birth to several new business schools, as well as transformed other research institutes. Contrary to the pursuit of general truths, the study of countries and international business appeared to legitimate the importance of the particular. No doubt, many of our colleagues stirred the embers of this fire by clinging fervently to the importance of international experience by which to understand this context.[2] In current parlance, international business tended to suggest that knowledge is 'situated'. Whereas this claim has a sound basis in the post-modernism of social studies, it is a linguistic turn that resulted in a language that few colleagues in business schools understood – to say the least!

There has been, in short, a curious stance that international business studies did not enjoy the same status of legitimacy as international studies have in social science disciplines. Increasingly, much of the functional content of international business has been absorbed by other fields. Whether international marketing or international finance, to choose two examples, has prospered within these functions is a question that I would answer largely in the negative. Moreover, one of the core aspects of international business has been the economics of the multinational enterprise which has a dubious status within international economics, despite the thoughtful and generous umbrella opened up by such scholars as Richard Caves. The cross-cultural field has been partly 'scientized' in organizational behaviour, while those who emphasize experience and context are still largely in the margins.

The most notable area of success has been the area of strategy and management, though the impact of international context and competition is largely absent in the thinking of many of the principal 'theorists' of this genre. To strategy theorists the recognition of the importance of context would be contrary to the effort of their notion of abstract theory. Thus, while grudging respect is given to field research on the multinational corporation, the strategy theorist's paranoia of appearing applied, especially given that strategy and management are applied fields, causes them to break into passive–aggressive hives.

There must be ways to resolve these many contradictions in the professional school of business. Herbert Simon offered one set of prescriptions by suggesting that professional schools should have 'design' as their task. Professional schools assume their professional responsibilities to the degree that they 'discover a science of design, a body of intellectually tough, analytic, partly formalizable, partly empirical, teachable doctrine about the design process'. From this suggestion, it is possible to understand such schools as places of exploration of the possible, not simply the analysis of the existing. Yet, the danger of heeding the first part of this prescription ('analytic') is that exploration lends itself to pure imagination. Once this guise is accepted, then it is easy to reject context ('empiric') or the world as distractions from theory.

It is here that Edward Carr is useful. In his short book entitled *What Is History?*, Edward Carr proposed that history is a dialogue between the past and present, between analysis and facts. Carr's proposal was a radical departure from the objectivist school of history and its insistence on truth. Since the present is ever-changing, so is history. In this sense, Carr anticipated the post-modern proclamation that research and the researcher are also 'situated'. This perspective shifted the focus, as Anthony Giddens would have said, from epistemology to ontology. We are no longer interested in truth so much as the understanding of the ontologies that we inhabit.

This is not a bad perspective for international studies which take context seriously. Carr's method is essentially constructionist, as subjective understandings are shared within a community that evaluates the truth claim of a history against the mustered facts. This constructive stance is a useful anecdote to the policy descriptions of 'science' that proposes normative advice on the basis of objectified findings. Such advice consists of statements that efficient firms focus on a single competence, or development requires open capital markets. Neither of these statements is universally true, both are contextually contingent, and yet substantial research has supported these claims.

It is a far more humble, yet honest, position to see research as a dialogue between facts – whether past or present – and our interpretations that are tested in a community of practising academics. This constructive perspective is not relativism, for not all views are equally valid. But neither is it objectivist, for claims to universalism cannot be made either.

There is the important question of whether we can evaluate the merits of a given community's research. This is not an easy question to answer, but in the context of applied domains, it is reasonable to ask if the community has contributed useful knowledge to external stakeholders. Carr suggests as well that history, because it is an ongoing dialogue, should be useful for the formation of policy. If the construction of economic knowledge is to be evaluated by criteria external to the self-referential norms of the community, we might, for example, ask has it contributed useful knowledge to the formation of economic policy? Does it provide clear prescription how to regulate monopoly powers in innovative industries? Does it provide workable models of how to build capitalist institutions in developing or transition economies?

We can similarly ask how well has international business responded to the external needs of its stakeholders. I am asking to hold in abeyance the evaluation of its research by its own internal criteria, and instead am posing the question 'How useful a field has it been?' In the language of Simon, we might ask if international business is a field of architectural design, would its house stand?

I propose that the answer is likely to be favourable because this dialogue of fact and interpretation has remained a core of the field's aesthetic values. It is a dialogue that has cost it a certain amount of legitimacy. I recall a colleague whom I held, and hold, in high esteem, looking at a paper filled with facts about the foreign direct investment and then blurt out in exasperation, 'why is international business so filled with numbers'? E. H. Carr provided the answer, namely, to have a dialogue between fact and interpretation (or more gracefully lauded as theory), both parties must be present at the table. How easy it is for theory when it does not have to bother with fact or context.

The claim I wish to make is that good empirics is good theory. The construction of artificial worlds does not invalidate the importance of validation. The prototype of the house, built in a 1 : 100 scale, may not be built, but if built, it would have to meet the physics of an actual world. This is the meaning of a world of design, as it is the constructionist agenda in admitting the collective dialogue of fact and interpretation.

As an illustration of how a definition of science can lead to bad architecture is an experience I had when requesting funding from the National Science Foundation. A number of years ago, Paul Almeida and I submitted a proposal to the NSF, asking for support for our project on the geographic basis of innovation and spillovers. We cited the inspirational work of Adam Jaffee, Manuel Trachtenberg and Rebecca Henderson who showed that important patents were more likely to be cited by patents filed by inventors in the same region than by inventors located in other regions. We proposed to investigate this claim by a detailed analysis of a single sector, semi-conductor design, with attention to regional differences. The NSF rejected the proposal, claiming that only cross-sectional work could validate general claims. We found alternative funding and the work was published, showing that spillovers exist but not for all regions; context matters. In 2004, the *American Economic Review* published a paper showing that the Jaffee, Trachtenberg and Henderson results do not hold for less aggregated data. The NSF would have done better if they funded several smaller studies – as we proposed – than asserting that science required universal results.

This Don Quixote adherence to universalism has resulted in many studies speaking badly to their questions. As odd as it may seem, we do not know in the year 2004 if foreign direct investment is good or bad for the world. I doubt very much if the question so posed is answerable. A contextual approach would try to understand the conditions under which direct investment is good (or bad). I do not rule out that this process might generate some broader assessment, though I am dubious. But the many studies sensitive to context – one thinks back to John Dunning's early work on direct investment in the UK or Raymond Vernon's work on American outward investment and its impact on the USA – are likely to form a more powerful dialogue between fact and interpretation useful for policy than an initial pursuit of general knowledge.

There is though a damning critique of the literature of international business of recent years: it has lost its engagement in the world. The important questions of globalization, the effects on development of multinational corporations, the transition in previously communist countries are largely absent from the main journals of international business. One offers the conjecture that the constant aggression of the insecure functional disciplines, and their claims to scientific generality, forced international business to synchronize into a common oscillation, much like crickets in the cold of the night. The journal pages are filled with articles complete with statistics and regressions. But are we asking the right and important questions? If we compare the questions of an earlier generation – can cross-cultural understanding be achieved, are multinational corporations good, have we narrowed our sights to smaller questions amenable to science but digressions from the more important issues of our time?

I started this essay in recognition that the internal validation of truth – subjectively but collectively held I have claimed – reflects an aesthetic. Equally, I have noted that self-referential dynamics of academic communities can drift toward research agendas and styles that reproduce but are potentially irrelevant. There is no doubt danger in foisting relevance a priori on a field. The only viable escape from this impasse for fields of professional design is the rendition of the dialogue between facts and interpretation as the central aesthetic of a community of academic practitioners.

The success of the field of international business, which is by no means minor, has rested on its ability to address important facts: how are multinational corporations operated, in what ways is meaning achieved between different cultures, what explains the country differences in economic behaviours? This is the legacy of the field that has been forgotten in all too many doctoral programmes that have tried to accommodate the claims of the administrative sciences. The survival of international business as an objective is a matter of sentiment. Its more compelling claim for our future investment is that it addresses the facts of our time to arrive at understanding the important questions of our world and the choices we have to make. It is a legacy that deserves to be remembered in our ambitions to create the dialogues that mark our present day.

Acknowledgement

My thanks to Peter Buckley for his invitation, despite all my hesitations.

Notes

1. There is the story of a meeting at the Santa Fe Institute in which the physicists were surprised at the mathematical formality of the economists; over time, formalism gave way to computation. See Anderson, P. W., K. J. Arrow, and D. Pines (eds) (1988) *The Economy as an Evolving Complex System*. Redwood City: Addison-Wesley.
2. Many of the early leaders in international business studies were former missionaries, or children of missionaries, or those with experience from American military engagements overseas. As children of the birth of the United Nations, they had a zealotry and commitment in international education that appeared apart from science.

5
Defining International Business through Its Research

Daniel P. Sullivan and John D. Daniels

Introduction

Leadership in knowledge production is vital to the ongoing success of an individual, organization or institution. Therefore, we believe that the question of 'What is international business (IB)?' is perhaps best answered by asking 'What knowledge do IB scholars seek, for what purpose, and why?' Thus, we focus our chapter on this question and organize it by categorizing the philosophical perspectives IB scholars use when seeking insightful and innovative interpretation of the knowledge they seek. Defining IB through its research is challenging, not only because of the scope of IB studies (they span all business functions and interact with a variety of non-business disciplines, thus we do not purport to be able either to describe the full array of IB topics, or to judge which have been most significant), but also because of the variety of philosophical perspectives one may use to organize an analysis (Sullivan, 1998). In recourse, we engage the omnibus terms scientific paradigm, humanist paradigm, and their combination (scientific humanist paradigm) to differentiate the different philosophical perspectives currently prevalent in IB. This categorization permits us to be consistent with Kuhn's observation (1990: 7) that 'Scientific development must be seen as a process driven from behind, not pulled from ahead – as evolution from, rather than evolution towards.' Further, although these perspectives share common ground, each also differs from one another with respect to topics studied, directions pursued, methods applied, results reported and paths proposed. Finally, this categorization permits us to reflect on existing IB research in terms of divergence and convergence, as well to ask the more provocative question, 'What might international business become?'

The scientific paradigm

The scientific paradigm (aka logical positivism or empiricism) has precise standards: the rational value of research depends on the formal validity or logic of its arguments, the accuracy of testing the arguments/theories as true or false, and the ease of replicating conclusions through independent empirical observations. A fundamental premise is that conditions exist prior to the theories developed to explain them. This paradigm sees the world as a well-behaved system of discrete parts operating in a consistent, systematic and predictable universe; it girds the idea that relationships between cause and effect are straightforward – e.g. 'if X, then Y'. Within this context, scientists assess objective data in order to predict the behaviour, control for anomalies and sustain system equilibrium. So predisposed, researchers reasonably aspire to know and understand all and ultimately specify universalistic and nomothetic knowledge – e.g. X per cent change in international activity for a firm will result in Y per cent change in performance. Fortified with a scientific outlook to search for general laws or rules, scholars seek the one best method that optimizes performance, i.e. Rugman's (1993: 87) thesis that MNEs have the 'single goal of efficient economic performance through a simplistic globalization strategy'.

In essence, the scientific paradigm is prescriptive; however, for the most part, IB prescriptions had to await descriptive research in order to create a common acceptance of terminology and a database from which scholars could examine patterns. Thus, IB research has been evolutionary and has linked scholars sequentially. For example, in the 1960s managers and the popular press began using terms (e.g. multinational, transnational) that the fledgling IB field needed to incorporate coherently; thus, in an early study, Ogram (1965) interviewed executives to determine collective definitions. Although these definitions have since evolved, they were a necessary precursor for ensuing research. The collection at Harvard, under the auspices of Raymond Vernon, of a database on large US companies' international operations spawned many dissertations that mined these data to discern international business patterns.

Two diverse examples, albeit simplified, should illustrate the link between descriptive and prescriptive IB studies. First, Robinson's (1964) historical description and explanation of developing countries' animosity toward inward FDI influenced models to predict expropriation (e.g. Knudsen, 1974), which, in turn, helped lead to studies of prescriptions for preventing expropriation (e.g. Bradley, 1977). Second, Friedmann and Kalmanoff's pioneering description of international joint ventures (1961) helped lead to descriptions of their problems (e.g. Franko, 1971) and finally to prescriptions for their success (e.g. Kumar and Seth, 1998).

Table 5.1 specifies several operating precepts of the scientific paradigm along with representative applied topics. Although a diverse literature, these studies share the premise that agents are rational actors that seek to optimize fulfilment of their objectives. This thesis shows up in any number of ways, from the notion of synoptic thought processes, objective specification schemas or precise relationships. This table highlights that IB research has focused on different agents, such as MNEs themselves or the country units with which they interact. Unquestionably, the scientific paradigm has made IB research more systematic. Researchers have collected objective data and refined our understanding of IB by accepting the premise that agents – whether workers, managers, companies, institutions or other stakeholders – are rational systems that operate as efficiently as possible. Buckley (2002) offers a case in point; he suggests that scientific efforts within the IB literature began with 'Dunning's (1958) meticulous analysis of US FDI in the UK (which) first systematised the industrial economics of foreign direct investment'. Further, the 2003 'Focused Issue' of *JIBS* on the 'The Future of the Multinational Enterprise: 25 Years Later' underscored the ongoing value of the scientific paradigm to the knowledge production in IB. By and large, these reports linked the foundation status of Buckley and Casson (1976) to its extensive use of systematic approaches and sophisticated statistical methods. Collectively, these reports underscore the application of the scientific paradigm to progressively more refined research designs, measures and analysis, which, in turn, supported the development of clearly defined laws, rules and principles of IB.

Table 5.1 The scientific paradigm of international business research: dimensions and examples

Dimension	Example
Identify the 'one best method' for performing a task in order to set a standard that imposes order, maximizes efficiency and optimizes performance	• The Globalization of Markets, Levitt, T., *Harvard Business Review*, 1983 • A Model of Balance of Payments Crises, Krugman, P., *Journal of Money, Credit, and Banking*, 1979 • Toward a Theory of the Universal Content and Structure of Values, Schwartz, S. and W. Bilsky, *Journal of Personality and Social Psychology*, 1990 • Towards a Capital Structure Theory for the Multinational Company, Eckert, S. and J. Engelhard, *Management International Review*, 1999 • The Six Major Puzzles in International Macroeconomics: Is There a Common Cause? Obstfeld and Rogoff, NBER 7777, 2000 • The Gains from International Trade, Once Again, Samuelson, P., *Economic Journal*, 1962
Specify procedures and tools to analyse, predict and control goals that then detail a decision-making discipline	• *Multinational Enterprise and Economic Analysis*, Caves, R., 1982 • A Rational Expectations Model of Financial Contagion, Kodres, L. and M. Pritsker, *Journal of Finance*, 2002 • Global Portfolio Planning and Market Interconnectedness, Douglas, S. and S. Craig, *Journal of International Marketing*, 1996 • Modal Choice in a World of Alliances: Analyzing Organizational Forms in the International Hotel Sector, Contractor, F. and S. Kundu, *Journal of International Business Studies*, 1998 • Interest Rates and Currency Prices in a Two-Country World, Lucas, R., *Journal of Monetary Economics*, 1982 • International Market Segmentation Based on Consumer-Product Relations, Hofstede, F., *Journal of Marketing Research*, 1999

Table 5.1   (Continued)

Dimension	Example
	• Seven Rules of International Distribution, Arnold, R. *Harvard Business Review*, 2000 • Models of Political Risk for Foreign Investment and Trade: an Assessment of Three Approaches, Llewellyn, H. and D. Chaddick, *Columbia Journal of World Business*, 1994 • A Model of Advertising Standardization in Multinational Corporations. Laroche, M. et al., *Journal of International Business Studies*, 2001
Develop perspectives that enable managers to reduce unpredictability and uncertainty systematically	• The Boundaries of Multinational Enterprises and the Theory of International Trade, Markusen, J. *Journal of Economic Perspectives*, 1995 • Rational Contagion and the Globalization of Securities Markets, Calvo and Mendoza, *Journal of International Economics*, June 2000 • Factors Influencing the Degree of International Pricing Strategy Standardization of Multinational Corporations, Theodosiou, M. and C. Katsikeas, *Journal of International Marketing*, 2001 • The Hierarchical Model of Market Entry Modes, Pan, Y. and D. Tse, *Journal of International Business Studies*, 2000 • The Effects of Strategy Type on the Market Orientation–Performance Relationship, Matsuno K. and J. Mentzer, *Journal of Marketing*, 2000 • Internal Financing of Multinational Subsidiaries: Debt vs. Equity, Chowdhry, B. and J. Coval, *Journal of Corporate Finance*, 1998 • Investor Diversification and International Equity Markets, French, K. and J. Poterba, *American Economic Review*, 1991 • International Investments and International Trade in the Product Life Cycle, Vernon, R. *Quarterly Journal of Economics*, 1966

Like any paradigm, the scientific perspective faces challenges. Its use of increasingly complex statistical techniques often proves to be ahistorical, decontextualized and reductionist. Its predisposition towards a binary logic of non-equivocating causality within a closed equilibrium context often suppresses other forms of reasoning that cannot be formally modelled (Safarian, 2003; Buckley and Casson, 2003). It also encourages precise modelling methods and tools to fit the presumed characteristics of the phenomena by excluding data mining to assess secondary and tertiary relationships. Finally, the scientific perspective is a closed rational approach, portraying agents in pursuit of preset ends, thereby disregarding likely connections to a wider environment.

The humanist paradigm

Within the milieu of IB studies, the assumptions of the scientific paradigm prove particularly troubling because of agents' cultural context, environments in which agents operate, and differences among agents, particularly MNEs, in terms of their unique combination of competencies. That is, the scientific paradigm assumes that (a) culture – namely values, expectations and motivations – is either exogenous or undifferentiated among clusters or countries, (b) workers, managers, companies, institutions and stakeholders aspire to optimize (usually economic) performance, and (c) what will work for one agent, such as one MNE, should work for another as well. Consequentially, the scientific paradigm neglects, if not rejects, the scope of the human element of IB studies. Against this backdrop, the humanist paradigm has steadily gained credibility within IB precisely because once these assumptions are questioned, as exemplified in Hofstede's (1983) milestone report that people with the same information might arrive at different decisions or behave dissimilarly because of their latent cultural values, then the universality of direct deductive inferences from the scientific paradigm becomes problematic. Therefore, the premise of cultural relativity, while meaning many things, ultimately rejects the premise that 'All agents rationally optimize performance.' This, in turn, casts doubt on the validity of the goal of the scientific paradigm to specify universalistic and nomothetic knowledge, i.e. not all stakeholders, depending on cultural conditions, necessarily accept a single goal to optimize performance, such as managers' 'single goal of efficient economic performance through a simplistic globalization strategy'.

Because of these shortcomings, scholars from any number of fields, including IB, have engaged an alternative paradigm, namely that of humanism. In contrast to the scientific paradigm, the humanist paradigm assumes there is no single best way to do anything because all things are relative. Generally, humanism is freely applied to modern doctrines and non-scientific techniques that presume the centrality of human experience – so-called anthropocentricity. Essentially, the humanist paradigm champions the idea that people and, by extension, organizational, institutional and national environments matter; hence, environmental relativity (especially culture) is a significant explanatory variable.

The humanist paradigm holds that coherence, not consistency, is the basis for relevance and validity. This principle moves interpretation from the absoluteness of the scientifically optimal method to that of the relative effectiveness of alternative approaches. As a growing number of comparative studies reported similarities and differences in behavioural, cognitive and latent constructs among countries, the thesis of cultural relativity and, hence, the humanist paradigm gained theoretical legitimacy.

The principles of the humanist paradigm have fundamentally affected the conceptualization, design and implementation of IB research. Table 5.2 shows a sample of representative topics, which have catalysed a host of issues and questions. Most immediately, they challenged prevailing ideas of human resource management, in particular its organizing assumption that one could reasonably assume a well-performing procedure, tool or even manager in Country X would function the same in Country Y. Instead, the humanist paradigm holds that the effectiveness of a particular managerial procedure, tool or practice is a function of its environment (Farmer and Richman, 1965). Moreover, success is not a function of a single best way but rather of continual improvement, itself a function of the intrinsic quest of people to imagine, question, create, learn and achieve. In following this reasoning, IB scholars have tried to assess if, when, how and why attitudes and values vary from one culture to another and what are the implications of variance to, for example, motivation, managerial work, expatriate performance, joint ventures, management practices, strategic alliances and so on.

Table 5.2 The humanist paradigm of international business research

Dimension	Example
Diversity in industries, markets, institutions and environments moderates the outlooks, attitudes and behaviours of agents	• The Cultural Relativity of Organizational Practices and Theories, Hofstede, G., *Journal of International Business Studies*, 1983 • *Development as Freedom*, Sen, A., 2000 • *Has Globalization Gone Too Far?* Rodrik, D., Institute for International Economics, 1997 • The Local and the Global: the Anthropology of Globalization and Transnationalism, *Annual Review of Anthropology*, 1995
Agents – whether affiliated with a company, market, country or collectivity – comprise a social community of people who have varying interests, rituals, habits and goals	• The Effect of National Culture on the Choice of Entry Mode, Kogut, B. and H. Singh, *Journal of International Business Studies*, 1988 • Converging Measurement of Horizontal and Vertical Individualism and Collectivism, Triandis, H. and J. Gelfand, *Journal of Personality and Social Psychology*, 1998 • What is a Global Manager?, Bartlett, C. and S. Ghoshal, *Harvard Business Review*, 1992
Motivation requires assigning roles and allocating responsibility in ways that fit latent outlooks and cognitive outlooks	• Culture and Congruence: the Fit between Management Practices and National Culture. Newman, K. and S. Nollen, *Journal of International Business Studies*, 1996 • The Impact of Values on Salespeople's Job Responses: a Cross-National Investigation. Dubinsky, A. et al., *Journal of Business Research*, 1997 • Organizational Motivation and the Global Concurrent Launch in Markets with Accelerated Technology, Li, T. et al., *International Business Review*, 2003 • Cultural Influences on Adaptation to Fluid Workgroups and Teams, Harrison, G. et al., *Journal of International Business Studies*, 2000 • Human Resource Management in Cross-Cultural Contexts: Emic Practices versus Etic Philosophies. Teagarden, M. and M. Glinow, *Management International Review*, 1997

Table 5.2   (Continued)

Dimension	Example
Cross-community variability moderates product concepts, consumer practices, industry conventions and market activities	• The Impact of Nationalism, Patriotism, and Internationalism on Consumer Ethnocentric Tendencies, Balabanis, G. et. al., *Journal of International Business Studies*, 2001 • Instituting the Marketing Concept in a Multinational Setting: the Role of National Culture, Nakata, C. and K. Sivakumar, *Journal of the Academy of Marketing Science*, 2001 • Will the Real World Citizen Please Stand Up: the Many Faces of Cosmopolitan Consumer Behavior, Cannon, H. and A. Yaprak, *Journal of International Marketing*, 2002

In essence, IB researchers noted early that the norms of business practices – e.g. human resource management, marketing, finance, production – vary substantially among countries. In this respect, most of the early publications were based on observation of a business function in a single country, such as Brazilian marketing (Taylor, 1965), or observational and anecdotal rather than measured (Hall, 1960). Based on these observations, various researchers questioned the universal applicability of business practices (Negandhi and Estafen, 1965; Negandhi and Prasad, 1971; Koontz, 1969). Others have measured and described companies' approaches to given situations, hypothesizing that variances are due either to the different environments in which they operate or to different internal characteristics for companies operating within the same environment. Finally, researchers following the humanism paradigm have been moving beyond observation by sampling representative groups to determine underlying causes of differences, such as those from the GLOBE study (House et al., 2002). In summary, humanistic research has described country and company differences and has sought to determine the extent of variances, why they exist, how they affect MNEs' and other stakeholders' performance, and how difficult they are to change.

Like its scientific counterpart, the humanist paradigm also suffers shortcomings. Most notably, there is scant research that links differences to performance by prescribing what agents should do – e.g. whether managers from cultures with norms of consultative management styles likely improve performance by being autocratic where autocratic management styles prevail. Consequently, the descriptive bent of comparative IB studies often results in stepchild findings, viewed sceptically by scholars and practitioners who prefer the decisive prescriptions (albeit often erroneous) that flow from scientific studies.

Interaction of paradigms: scientific humanism

The growing exchange of ideas between the scientific and humanist paradigms in IB has helped make 'scientific' research more scientific. Increased application of ideas from the behavioural sciences, like anthropology and social psychology, to analyse the actions of and relationships among agents and stakeholders has improved the rigour of scientific interpretation. In other words, the interaction has resulted in more realistic assumptions and has moved much IB research from 'If X, then Y' to 'If X, then Y or Z depending on the people and circumstances involved'. For example, Chui et al. (2002) found that adding the dimensions of national conservatism and mastery to traditional economic and institutional variables led to more accurate prediction of the capital structures that companies employ. Further, recent studies of joint ventures have included variables such as trust and personal attachment to help explain both the propensity for shared ownership and the performance of joint ventures (i.e. Makino and Neupert, 2000; Luo, 2002). Thus, one would not be too far adrift, as seen in Table 5.3, to characterize a growing number of contemporary IB studies as examples of 'scientific humanism'.

Synthesis or hegemony?

The linking of the scientific and humanism paradigms presumes an open and equal exchange of ideas between them. While synthesis is an appealing scenario, we increasingly believe otherwise. Rather than the fusion of equals, we see the philosophical hegemony of the scientific paradigm as it co-opts 'useful' principles from the humanist paradigm but does not reset its standards of predictive success, analytical intelligibility and methodological precision. Certainly,

Table 5.3 The scientific humanism paradigm of international business research

Dimension	Examples
Systematic integration of the objective principles of the scientific perspective with the subjective sensitivity of the humanist perspective to study the actions of and relationships among agents	• The Eclectic (OLI) Paradigm of International Production: Past, Present and Future, Dunning, J., *International Journal of the Economics of Business,* 2001 • *Globalization and its Discontents,* Stiglitz, J., 2002 • *The Global Economy and the Nation State,* Drucker, P. Foreign Affairs, 1997 • *Global Trade and Conflicting National Interests,* Gomory, R. and W. Baumol, 2000 • *The Competitive Advantage of Nations,* Porter, M. 1990
Complementing and contrasting the explanatory power of the scientific and humanist perspectives to improve analysis of the rational and behavioural properties of the phenomenon	• National Culture, Transaction Costs, and the Choice between Joint Venture and Wholly Owned Subsidiary, Makino, S. and K. Neupert, *Journal of International Business Studies,* 2000 • The Determination of Capital Structure: Is National Culture a Missing Piece to the Puzzle? Chui, A. et al., *Journal of International Business Studies,* 2002 • A Multilevel Approach to Trust in Joint Ventures, Currall, S. and A. Inkpen. *Journal of International Business Studies,* 2002 • Effects of Nationality on Global Strategy, Yip, G. et al., *Management International Review,* 1997 • On Cross-Country Differences in the Persistence of Real Exchange Rates, Cheung, Y. and K. Lai, *Journal of International Economics,* 2000 • Global Mindsets and Cognitive Shifts in a Complex Multinational Corporation, Murtha, T. et al., *Strategic Management Journal,* 1998 • The Impact of National Culture and Economic Ideology on Managerial Work Values, Ralston, D. et al., *Journal of International Business Studies,* 1997

	• Business and Social Networks in International Trade, Rauch, J., *Journal of Economic Literature*, 2000
Specification and application of dynamic modelling techniques to elaborate the standards of validity	• Using Neural Network Analysis to Uncover the Trace Effects of National Culture, Veiga, J. et al., *Journal of International Business Studies*, 2000
	• Relationship Bonding and Trust as a Foundation for Commitment in U.S.– Mexican Strategic Alliances: a Structural Equation Modeling, Rodriguez, C. and D. Wilson, *Journal of International Marketing*, 2002
	• Firm Productivity and Export Markets: a Non-Parametric Approach, Delgado, M., et al., *Journal of International Economics*, 2002
	• Countries and their Products: a Cognitive Structure Perspective, Shimp, T. et al., *Journal of the Academy of Marketing Science*, 1993
	• Nonlinear Systems Theory: a More Dynamic Approach to International Strategic Management, Martinez, Z. et al., *Managerial Finance*, 1999
	• International Business Cycles with Endogenous Incomplete Markets, Kehoe, P. and F. Perri, *Econometrica*, 2000

various applications of the humanist paradigm have demonstrated that they are as rigorous as their scientific counterparts – provided their rigour is judged by criteria that are markedly different from those used in conventional empirical research. If not, then objective standards predictably trump subjective interpretations.

Consider, as an example, the 'acceptance' of the legitimacy of humanist research in the IB field. Although there are early exemplars of such research, many IB scholars with a scientific bent did not judge it credible until Hofstede's (1983) study applied a scientific epistemology replete with conventional sampling, data collection and statistical standards as opposed to relying on a forceful interpretive inquiry. Ensuing works by like-minded 'scientific' scholars showed that humanist research could be conducted within traditions that were decidedly positivistic. Indeed, a substantial body of research in the social sciences – notably in political science, economics, management, sociology and organization studies – illustrates the application of non-quantitative methods within traditional positivistic assumptions about the nature of reality and the production of knowledge. Concomitantly, one can link much of the prestige and power of IB research to scholars' success in designing and reporting such research (Brock, 2003). Thus, the question of what is IB, from a philosophical frame, is presently best defined in terms of the hegemonic fusion of the scientific paradigm with its humanist counterpart. This 'merger' has helped IB develop a coherent and realistic research outlook that aspires to support cross-functional and cross-disciplinary research.

Current sentiments and situations in IB and the world, however, suggest that the scientific humanist paradigm is increasingly inadequate. The emergence of an arguably extraordinary environment of globalization elicits calls for transforming our idea of what international business is and, more significantly, must become. Put differently, notwithstanding the robustness of the scientific humanist paradigm, its continued dependence on assumptions that reality is concrete, separate from researchers, and understandable through ostensibly objective empiricism limits its meaningful application to fewer and fewer IB phenomena.

More specifically, consider Buckley's (2002) suggestion that, following decades of great accomplishment, the 'international business research agenda is running out of steam'. Worse still, Buckley contends that the discipline presently lacks an apparent sense of purpose to galvanize effort. This limitation is further complicated by the emergence of agents and activities, i.e. as Buckley identifies, 'mergers and acquisitions, knowledge management, geography, location, globalization, and new institutions such as NGOs', that defy, if not reject, analysis within a scientific humanist paradigm. Granted, these sorts of phenomena possess both rational and behavioural properties that fall within the ontological and epistemological parameters of existing paradigms. However, they increasingly manifest properties and tendencies that challenge our efforts to design, anchor and report meaningful research of them.

If, in fact, gaps grow between reality and our notions of what IB is, then regaining relevance moves us to more pointedly ask, 'what must IB become?' We believe that the onus falls upon IB scholars to identify new possibilities to discriminate issues, classify variables, organize analysis and anchor abstractions in ways that produce useful knowledge that speaks to various stakeholders. Returning to Kuhn's (1990, p. 7) notion that scientific development is 'evolution from, rather than evolution towards' provides some guidance. Put simply, what IB is and must become is easily defined yet arduously achieved. Regarding the former, IB must evolve toward fountainheads of ideas that enrich and elaborate the scientific and humanist paradigms in ways that improve the meaningfulness of IB research (Toyne and Nigh, 1997; Mendenhall, 1999). Regarding the latter, IB must become a discipline that aggressively encourages the breach of some intellectual boundaries set around its paradigmatic schema of scientific humanism. Scholars have the obligation, if intent on maintaining the vibrancy of IB as a concept, discipline and institution, to refuse to be confined, regulated and disciplined by increasingly anachronistic notions of scientific positivism – be it quantitative or qualitative. Scholars and managers alike must adopt the perspectives that create the tools to function in dynamic and complex environments, applying cross-functional and cross-disciplinary approaches to model agents, their activities and interlocking systems as they are, not as we wish them to be.

The dynamic of evolution

IB studies, like many disciplines, face the challenge of reaffirming relevance or fading away. Fortunately, IB scholars have successfully met this challenge in the past. For example, reflections in the 2003 'Focused Issue' of *JIBS* on the 'The Future of the Multinational Enterprise: 25 Years Later' suggest the likely dynamic of change. Throughout this issue, there is a sense of the Zeitgeist of IB 25 years ago. Specifically, Safarian (2003, p. 123) recounts that IB was a 'field in ferment' in the 1960s and 1970s, following 'two decades of experimentation with a variety of approaches'. Within this context, Buckley and Casson's (2003, p. 219) avowedly positivist approach to use statistics to 'reveal the underlying dynamics of multinational behavior' established 'the right theory [whereby] it would be possible to use the statistics to pass judgment on competing views'. These ideas evolved into the scientific paradigm, whose 'unifying set of ideas, analytical power, institutional focus, and methodological accessibility' appealed to the then loosely related areas of IB studies (Safarian, 2003, p. 116). Successful applications progressively legitimated IB studies.

We believe this dynamic of change is set to replay – albeit under different intellectual circumstances – by applying the precepts and procedures of novel paradigms and integrating these findings into the mainstream IB literature. Precedence suggests that IB scholars have the capacity to derive the needed insights to navigate the future. Recall IB's adoption of the humanist paradigm and the adaptation of it to the scientific paradigm. This adoption was not a preordained outcome. Other fields, notably economics and political science, continue to struggle with the humanist paradigm's scepticism of rationality and optimization. In fact, IB may command a distinctive competence to manage this evolution; historically the field has been more cross-functional and cross-disciplinary than other business fields. Thus, as exemplified by the very thesis of this text, IB researchers may intuitively understand how, as well as be intellectually more predisposed, to breach the intellectual boundaries (see also Dunning, 1989; Daniels, 1991; Toyne and Nigh, 1997; Buckley, 2002; Buckley and Casson, 2003).

References

Bradley, D. (1977) 'Managing against Expropriation', *Harvard Business Review*, July–August: 75–83.

Brock, J. K. (2003) 'The "Power" of International Business Research', *Journal of International Business Studies*, 34 (1): 90–9.

Buckley, P. J. and Casson, M. (1976) *The Future of the Multinational Enterprise*. London: Macmillan – now Palgrave Macmillan.

Buckley, P. J. (2002) 'Is the International Business Research Agenda Running out of Steam?', *Journal of International Business Studies*, 33(2): 365–74.

Buckley, P. J. and Casson, M. (2003) 'The Future of the Multinational Enterprise in Retrospect and in Prospect', *Journal of International Business Studies*, 34 (2): 219–23.

Chui, A. Lloyd, A. and C. Y. Kwok (2002) 'The Determination of Capital Structure: Is National Culture a Missing Piece to the Puzzle?', *Journal of International Business Studies*, 33(1): 99–128.

Daniels, J. D. (1991) 'Relevance in International Business Research. A Need for More Linkages', *Journal of International Business Studies*, 22: 177–86.

Dunning, J. H. (1958) *American Investment in British Manufacturing Industry*. London: George Allen and Unwin.

Dunning, J. H. (1989) 'The Study of International Business: a Plea for a More Interdisciplinary Approach', *Journal of International Business Studies*, 20: 411–36.

Farmer, R. N. and Richman, B. M. (1965) *Comparative Management and Economic Progress*. Homewood, Ill.: Richard D. Irwin.

Franko, Lawrence G. (1971) *Joint Venture Survival in Multinational Corporations*. New York: Praeger.

Friedmann, W. and G. Kalmanoff (1961) *Joint International Business Ventures*. New York: Columbia University Press.

Hall, E. T. (1960) 'The Silent Language in Overseas Business', *Harvard Business Review*, May–June.

Hofstede, G. (1983) 'The Cultural Relativity of Organizational Practices and Theories', *Journal of International Business Studies*, 14: 75–89.

House, R. et al., (2002) 'Understanding Cultures and Implicit Leadership Theories across the Globe', *Journal of World Business*, 37: 3–10.

Knudsen, H. (1974) 'Explaining the National Propensity to Expropriate: an Ecological Approach', *Journal of International Business Studies*, Spring, 51–72.

Koontz, H. (1969) 'A Model for Analyzing the Universality of Management', *Academy of Management Journal*, December, 415–29.

Kuhn, T. S. (1970) *The Structure of Scientific Revolutions*, 2nd edn. University of Chicago Press, Chicago.

Kuhn, T. S. (1990) 'The Road since Structure', *PSA*, 2(7): 3–13.

Kumar, S. and A. Seth (1998) 'The Design of Coordination and Control Mechanisms for Managing Joint Venture Relationships', *Strategic Management Journal*, 19(6): 579–99.

Luo, Y. (2002) 'Stimulating Exchange in International Joint Ventures: an Attachment-Based View', *Journal of International Business Studies*, 33(1): 169–82.

Makino, S. and K. Neupert (2000) 'National Culture, Transaction Costs, and the Choice between Joint Venture and Wholly Owned Subsidiary', *Journal of International Business Studies*, 31(4): 705–14.

Mendenhall, M. E. (1999) 'On the Need for Paradigmatic Integration in International Human Resource Management', *Management International Review*, 39(3): 65–87.

Negandhi, A. and B. D. Estafen (1965) 'A Research Model to Determine the Applicability of American Know-How in Differing Cultures and/or Environments', *Academy of Management Journal*, December, 309–18.

Negandhi, A. R. and S. B. Prasad (1971) *Comparative Management*. New York: Apple-Century-Crofts.

Ogram, E. W., Jr (1965). *The Emerging Pattern of the Multinational Corporation*. Atlanta: Georgia State University Bureau of Business Research.

Robinson, R. D. (1964) *International Business Policy*. New York: Holt, Rinehart and Winston.

Rugman, A. (1993) 'Drawing the Border for a Multinational Enterprise and a Nation State', in Lorraine Eden and Evan Potter (eds), *Multinationals in the Global Political Economy*, New York: St. Martin's Press.

Safarian, A. (2003) 'Internalization and the MNE: a Note on the Spread of Ideas', *Journal of International Business Studies*, 34(2): 117–26.

Sullivan, D. (1998) 'Cognitive Tendencies in International Business Research: Implications of a "Narrow Vision"', *Journal of International Business Studies*, 29 (4): 837.

Taylor, D. (1965) 'Marketing in Brazil', *Proceedings of the American Marketing Association*, 114.

Toyne, B. and Nigh, D. (1997) *International Business: an Emerging Vision*. Columbia, SC: The University of South Carolina Press.

6

The Institutional Environment for International Business

Witold J. Henisz

International business is the study of transactions between counter-parties who either reside in different nations or who reside in one nation but are compared to a pair of counterparties in another nation. This simple definition focuses our attention on the key facet of research in this area that distinguishes it from other fields. International business research necessarily requires attention to the institutional characteristics that alter the costs of engaging in business activity of a given form in one nation as compared to another. In this chapter, I examine the nature of these differences in the institutional environment and their implications for the current and future state of international business research.

Scholars in the field of international business base their research largely in the disciplines of economics and sociology. The study of actual business activity precludes the simplifying assumptions of perfect rationality among atomistic agents interacting in a world where complete contingent claims contracts are feasible as well as abstraction from the underlying economic motivation for the creation and maintenance of relationships between actors. The extension of this study to international business similarly precludes the simplifying assumption that the local institutional context equally supports all forms of business activity regardless of the type of technology, the identity of the investors, the mode of organization and the relationship between the investors and the host-country government and, more broadly, its polity. Thus the study of business activity which is already an inherently interdisciplinary activity concerning the organization of economic activity among individuals grouped in teams, firms, alliances and networks now spans the disciplinary boundary of political science as well.

The first insight deriving from this integration is the importance of differences in local institutional contexts for core questions of international business including the determinants of investment location, organization and performance. Based on a review of this literature, one might conclude that the field of international business research has successfully incorporated and contributed to state-of-the-art disciplinary research regarding the importance of national institutional context for economic activity.

If we accept that managers and researchers should be interested in not only cross-sectional but also time series variation in institutional context, however, confidence regarding successful contribution to and even integration of disciplinary work rapidly breaks down. The second body of work that I review draws largely from the disciplines of political economy with limited applications to international business. This literature examines the determinants of change in the local institutional context. Such capabilities while always of strategic value are of particular importance for international business as the ability of organizations to predict, plan for and adapt to such change both influences the ability of an organization to select, organize and attain peak performance across the portfolio of local institutional contexts that they face and also assists an organization within a given institutional context particularly when, as is often the case, institutional change is more prevalent in the host country than the home country market.

The impact of institutional context on entry, entry mode and exit[1]

To successfully deploy its resources in a new country, a multinational firm must identify and contend with numerous differences between the host country market and the markets in which it has previously operated (Beamish, 1988; Hymer, 1976; Martin et al., 1998; Zaheer, 1995). A recent study that examined regulations of entry in 75 countries found that the official procedures and costs required to start a new business varied from as few as 2 procedures (Canada) taking 2 days (Canada) and 0.4 per cent of average per capita income (New Zealand) to as many as 20 procedures (Bolivia) requiring up to 174 days

(Mozambique) and 263 per cent of average per capita income (Bolivia) (Djankov et al., 2000). Such differences may be the result of differences in the relative costs of contracting for the acquisition of needed factors of production or for downstream sales (Fisman and Khanna, 1998; Granovetter, 1995; Khanna, 2000; Khanna and Palepu, 1998, 1999, 2000a, b, c; Khanna and Rivkin, 2000; Nee, 1992), the protection of intellectual property (Lee and Mansfield, 1996; Oxley, 1999), the payment of taxes (Grubert and Mutti, 1991; Harris et al., 1993; Hines, 1998), the acquisition of government licences and the payment of fees, the prevalence of corruption (Wei, 2000) and the means and feasibility of exit. Even where laws and regulations appear similar, differences in legal systems can have important differences in such relevant outcomes as the protection afforded to shareholders versus creditors or minority investors (La Porta et al., 1998, 1999).

Cultural differences between nations also can influence multinational entry strategies. For example, substantial evidence of cross-national differences in such factors as 'administrative practices and employee expectations' (Kogut and Singh, 1988, p. 414) or the adoption of three paradigms of organizational management: scientific management, human relations and structural analysis (Guillén, 1994), illustrate the difficulty with which models of management are transferred from one nation to another (Guillén, 2001). Empirical evidence supporting these differences is found in the studies of Hamilton and Biggart (1988) on the industrial arrangements and organizational strategies employed in the economies of South Korea, Taiwan and Japan, and in Biggart and Guillén (1999) who looked at the evolution of the auto industry in South Korea, Taiwan, Spain and Argentina.

Institutional differences between nations magnify difficulties in collecting, interpreting and organizing the relevant information necessary to mount a successful entry. Markets that are similar in political structure, factor market structure or culture pose less uncertainty, relatively lower costs of entry and, therefore, lower hurdle rates of return. Investors are hence more likely to enter countries where the future policy regime is relatively easy to predict (Bennet and Green, 1972; Gastanaga et al., 1998; Green and Cunningham, 1975; Henisz and Delios, 2001; Loree and Guisinger, 1995; Root and Ahmed, 1978; Stobaugh, 1969; Vernon, 1977; Wei, 2000). Relatedly, investors are more likely to enter countries that are culturally similar, and have similar organizational structures (Hanson, 1999; Loree and Guisinger, 1995).

The impact of institutions on entry strategies can extend beyond the choice of where to invest to include the design of local operations. For example, firms that perceive hazards emanating from policy uncertainty can take hazard-mitigating actions designed to shift the decision calculus of the potential expropriating government. Such a shift should seek to either raise the political and/or economic costs (lost revenue, employment and future investment) to asset or revenue expropriation, or lower the benefits (the value of seized assets or revenue stream and the nationalist political reaction) from expropriation.

As an example of a hazard-mitigating strategy, a multinational can form a partnership with a host country firm. In such a partnership, the host country firm would also suffer in the event of an expropriation of a foreign subsidiary's returns or its assets because of the subsidiary's dependence on a continuing relationship with its parent firms for its complementary assets. In exchange for ownership in the foreign subsidiary, a host country partner provides a valuable service. Host country firms tend to use, on average, a greater percentage of domestic inputs. Because of superior information regarding the availability of, terms of and procedures for acquiring goods in the domestic market, host country partners rely more heavily than the multinational on domestically sourced labour, intermediate products and trading partners. While a multinational may pay to acquire this form of local information, pursuing such a strategy raises production costs relative to domestic firms.

Depending on the size of this cost wedge, a multinational shifts some positive quantity of inputs from domestic to international sourcing. Expropriation of the assets or revenue stream of a joint venture between a multinational and a host country partner will therefore result in a greater expropriation of assets or revenue streams owned by domestic constituents than expropriation of a solely foreign venture. As more domestic constituents are implicated in the expropriation, a partnership between a multinational and a host country firm is, on average, politically more costly to expropriate for the government than a solely foreign venture.[2] Gatignon and Anderson (1988), Hill et al. (1990), Agarwal and Ramaswami (1992), Oxley (1999), Delios and Beamish (1999), Smarzynska and Wei (2000) and Henisz (2000) provide empirical evidence supporting this link between market entry mode choice and the degree of policy uncertainty.[3] Similarly, Goodnow and Hansz (1972), Davidson and McFetridge (1985), Kogut and Singh (1988) and Erramilli (1996) find an analogous link between cultural proximity and the choice of entry mode.

A growing body of work examines the organizational strategies adopted by local firms to surmount the 'institutional voids' present in many institutional contexts. In the absence of such specialized market-intermediating institutions in the realms of financial, labour and product markets, local firms may follow one of three strategies. First, they may increase their horizontal scope in business group structures so to share these intermediating functions within a loosely coupled organizational rubric commonly referred to as a business group. Khanna and Palepu (2000c) find a diversification premium in the Indian context where intermediate markets are relatively under-developed. Chang and Hong (2000) use a more direct test of the benefits of internalizing missing markets by demonstrating perform-ance benefits to Korean *chaebol* that share financial and intangible assets. Exploiting variation in missing markets within a country over time as opposed to internalization across firms within a country, Khanna and Palepu (2000b) demonstrate that the performance benefits associated with group membership decline over time in Chile during a period in which intermediate markets were developing rapidly. Foley (2001) uses a similar set of arguments to argue that multinational corporations are able to use internal capital, labour and intangible assets to surmount host-market inefficiencies in those markets.

Second, they may cluster geographically to provide incentives for specialized private intermediaries to develop locally despite their general absence from the national economy. By collocating, a group of firms may create economic incentives for specialist intermediaries to develop. Michael Porter (1998, 2000) has recently advocated the development of such clusters as a development strategy for emerging economies.

Finally, they may seek ties to intermediating institutions in other countries either directly (i.e. accessing foreign capital or labour mar-kets) or indirectly (i.e. by allying with foreign firms). Guillén (2000) argues that business group structures are particularly beneficial when government policies limit access to key resources either domestically or internationally and finds support for this hypothesis across a sample of nine emerging markets. Siegel (2003) finds that local firms with political connections of particular importance in the current Korean political context are dramatically more likely to form alliances with US, European and Japanese multinationals. Siegel (2002) considers the reputation effects of listing an ADR on the New York Stock Exchange. The requisite information or capabilities may also be present within the focal firm as evidenced by the results of Delios and Henisz (2003b) who find that firms with more experience in countries with high political hazards are less sensitive to such hazards in their entry decisions. Henisz (2003) develops the arguments for the existence of political hazard-mitigating capabilities more fully in the context of private investment in electricity generation.

In addition to organizational characteristics, the type of assets chosen for overseas investment may vary across different institutional structures. Empirical work that has adopted a case study approach provides strong support for the hypothesis that long-lived and/or politically visible investments such as those in infrastructure sectors will be particularly sensitive to a country's institutional environment (Bergara Duque et al., 1998; Caballero and Hammour, 1998; Crain and Oakley, 1995; Dailami and Leipziger, 1998; Daniels and Trebilcock, 1994; Grandy, 1989; Levy and Spiller, 1994; Levy and Spiller, 1996; Ramamurti, 1996; Savedoff and Spiller, 1997; Spiller and Vogelsang, 1996; Williamson, 1976). Two recent efforts to extend this logic to panel datasets in telecommunications (Henisz and Zelner, 2001) and electricity (Henisz and Zelner, 2002) have also found strong support for the hypothesis that political institutions that fail to constrain arbitrary behaviour by political actors dampen the incentive for infrastructure providers to deploy capital and, *ceteris paribus*, yield lower levels of per capita infrastructure investment.

The sequence of investment within a country may also vary in the institutional environment. Delios and Henisz (2003a) argue that the internationalization's literature assumptions regarding the evolution of investment types proceeding from a sales subsidiary to a joint venture to a wholly owned manufacturing facility is contingent upon the primary source of uncertainty being derived from the marketplace as opposed to the policymaking process. Where the latter dominates, the hazard-mitigating benefits of local production as opposed to local competition argue for reversing this order and beginning the within-country sequence of investment with a manufacturing facility.

Regardless of the entry mode or type, unstable policy regimes and culturally dissimilar markets are likely associated with performance penalties relative to their more stable or familiar counterparts. Carroll and Delacroix (1982) find higher mortality rates for newspapers in Argentina and Ireland during periods of political unrest. Zaheer and Mosakowski (1997) find that the failure rates of foreign firms in the financial service sector are higher in more tightly regulated and less globally integrated markets. Li and Guisinger (1991) find an analogous relationship between cultural proximity and survival as do Barkema et al. (1996) and Barkema and Vermeulen (1997).

Institutional change and international business

Given the importance of the formal and informal institutional context for the location, organization and performance of international business activity, managers must concern themselves not only with variation in that institutional structure across countries but also across time. Specifically, investors often need to understand not only the current institutional structure and its stability over time but also its likely path of evolution. Managers must be able to unpack the policymaking process and identify the key interest groups and coalitions that interact within the formal political structures to militate for change. Broadly, the relevant literature that examines this question can be broken down into two components which emphasize, respectively, the supply and demand sides of the process. Efforts to bring these literatures together particularly in an empirical context are extremely limited and scarcer still if that context is limited to one in which economic actors are centrally implicated. As a result, my review will largely focus on identifying key findings in the relevant disciplines and their potential impact on current research in international business.

Supply-side constraints on institutional change

On the supply side of the process, a growing body of literature linking political institutions and economic outcomes has asked whether institutions that offer 'some credible restrictions on the state's ability to manipulate economic rules to the advantage of itself and its constituents' (North and Weingast, 1989, p. 808) can overcome what Weingast has labelled 'the fundamental political dilemma of an economic system'. Namely, 'a government strong enough to protect property rights is also strong enough to confiscate the wealth of its citizens' (Weingast, 1993).

That confiscation may take the form of outright expropriation of assets or of a revenue stream from those assets but more commonly involves changes in the policy regime that intentionally or unintentionally have the result of altering the value of the revenue stream generated by private sector assets. Examples include changes in tax policy, regulations or procedural requirements. While such actions are often far removed from the expropriation of property, plant and equipment, they still impact the decisions of private actors especially those that include long-lived up-front investments with substantially reduced value in their next best use (Pindyck, 1991).

An important early contribution to our understanding of how political institutions can provide a credible commitment to property rights comes from the work of positive political theorists such as Thomas Gilligan and Keith Krehbiel (1980) and Kenneth Shepsle and Barry Weingast (1987) who examined the role of the committee structure of the US Congress in controlling the problem of voting cycles (Riker, 1980) expected in a democratic legislature. The property rights in question were political rather than economic but the principle that the structure of political institutions affects policy outcomes extends far beyond the Washington beltway. In order to identify the reasons underlying the much observed and often described existence of committee power, these theorists diverged from the case study approach of earlier literature and adopted simple spatial models of political interaction to derive structure-induced equilibria in the political process. They demonstrate the importance of the agenda setting and last-mover rights held by the committees in the determination of policy outcomes. They tested their theoretical framework by predicting and testing for shifts in policy outcomes after shifts in majorities on relevant committees (Gilligan et al., 1989; Shepsle, 1986; Weingast, 1981, 1984; Weingast and Marshall, 1988; Weingast and Moran, 1983).

Subsequent work in the field of positive political theory has built outward from these simple early models to test for the relative importance of these and other hypotheses[4] on the structure of Congressional committees (Groseclose, 1994a, b); and to incorporate other political actors including the President (Ferejohn and Charles, 1990; Gely and Spiller, 1990; Spiller and Gely, 1992), bureaucracies

(Gely and Spiller, 1990; McNollGast, 1987, 1989; Schwartz et al., 1994; Spiller, 1990; Spiller and Gely, 1992) and the courts (Cameron et al., 2000; de Figueiredo and Tiller, 1996; Gely and Spiller, 1990, 1992; Songer et al., 1994, 1995; Spiller, 1992; Spiller and Gely, 1992; Spiller and Tiller, 1996, 1997). More recently, a few authors have taken preliminary steps to extend the spatial modelling of political action to political systems outside the United States (Baron, 1998; Bawn, 1999; Bottom et al., 2000, Moe and Caldwell, 1994; Mueller and Pareira, 1999; Palmer, 1995; Ramseyer and Rasmusen, 2001; Spiller and Vogelsang, 1996) or to multilateral bargaining games (Butler and Hauser, 2000; Kreppel, 2000; Richards, 1999; Tsebelis and Garrett, 2000).

The primary result from this literature is that policy outcomes are a function of political structure. The possession of veto power over a final outcome is among the most important of the structures under study as it limits the range of discretion by other political actors. Specifically, any single actor with authority to set policy acts knowingly that the final policy outcome must be within a range of policies that satisfies all actors with veto power. Therefore, rational behaviour dictates the choice of the most preferred policy not subject to a veto.

This logic is the basis for an analysis of cross-nation variation in political institutions used to predict variation in the investment and profitability of telecommunications companies in a series of case studies assembled in Levy and Spiller (1996). The authors isolate a small set of institutional variables that, across their sample of five countries, explain much of the variation in firm performance.

First, in the absence of an independent judiciary (one whose authority over contracts between private and public entities is not subject to political intervention), governments are unable credibly to commit without external assistance. Any promise, legislation, contract or rule can easily be reneged upon without the recourse of an appeal to an independent party.[5] Such societies, which include absolutist monarchies, centrally planned economies and single-party totalitarian states can be characterized by Louis XIV's famous dictum 'L'état, c'est moi'.[6] By contrast, the existence of an independent judiciary gives citizens and firms an independent forum to which they can appeal arbitrary, capricious or self-serving rulings by the state and whose own rulings they may have confidence will be enforced by that state. Levy and Spiller (1994) point out that, in the absence of judicial independence, efforts at establishing judicial reform should precede efforts at privatization or, if privatization must be enacted for political reasons, governments should rely on third-party commitment mechanisms such as those provided by multilateral institutions.

A related line of inquiry emphasizes the preference dispersion of actors within a given veto player. For example, the work of George Tsebelis concludes 'the potential for policy change decreases with the number of veto players, the lack of congruence (dissimilarity of policy positions among veto players) and the cohesion (similarity of policy positions among the constituent units of each veto player)' (Tsebelis, 1995). Thus the existence of an institutionally independent actor with the ability to act as a check on its peers is less relevant for investors where the preferences of the actor that inhabit that institution overlap with the preferences of the actors that it purportedly checks. Such overlap may be expected in cases where one body elects or appoints the other such as is the case for the executive in a Westminster Parliamentary government or regulatory or judicial actors that serve at the pleasure of the current executive. Electoral rules that influence the composition of political actors relative to the polity are also relevant in this regard.

These theoretical insights are supported by a number of empirical studies that examine the responsiveness of policies to certain exogenous shifts in the economic or policy environment or examine long-term trends in fiscal or monetary policy. For example, Hallerberg and Basinger (1998) find that in response to the policy innovation of tax cuts enacted by the United States in the 1980s, other OECD nations with few de facto veto points lowered their tax rates by a greater amount than countries with a larger number of such checks and balances. Franzese (1999) and Treisman (2000) find that countries with more veto points have stable levels (either high or low) of government deficits and inflation respectively. The vast literature on political determinants of budget deficits (see Persson and Tabellini, 1999 for a recent review) that posits that countries with a larger number of policymakers will have a more difficult time allocating costs (tax revenue) but will be more likely to generate policy logrolls that increase spending (expenditure) and thus generate larger deficits is also consistent with the underlying logic presented here especially to the extent that it isolates the fiscal response to exogenous shocks (Alt and Lowry, 1994; Persson, 2001; Poterba, 1994; Roubini and

Sachs, 1989).[7] Henisz (2004) builds upon this prior research set primarily in OECD countries by showing that across a sample of as many as 92 countries over as many as 23 years, checks and balances are negatively associated with the volatility of fiscal policy.

Institutional development may directly reduce uncertainty over the future policy regime and provide investors with recourse in the event of arbitrary or capricious behaviour thus encouraging investment, but there are also several plausible indirect channels leading from better developed institutional structures to more favourable policy outcomes. These include fostering the development of a strong and independent press (Dyck and Zingales, 2001), an improvement in the availability and efficiency of provision of public goods (Boix, 2001; Esfahani and Ramirez, 1999; Roller and Waverman, 2001; Tanzi and Davoddi, 1997), curtailment of corruption possibly through better monitoring and enforcement (Mauro, 1997; Tanzi and Davoddi, 1997), better rather than more stable or predictable economic policies (Ahn and Hemmings, 2000; Collier and Gunning, 1999; Frankel and Romer, 1996; Nelson and Singh, 1998; Sachs and Warner, 1995) and financial market development (Bekaert et al., 2001; Levine et al., 2000; Levine and Zervos, 1998; Rajan and Zingales, 1998).

The dramatic progress of this literature in international political economy points to a gap in the analogous literature in international business. As surveyed in the previous section, researchers have increasingly acknowledged the importance of the political process for entry and organizational decisions as well as performance outcomes. That acknowledgement of importance has not, however, kept up with the theoretical and empirical advances in conceptualization and measurement of the institutional environment. Rather than continue to use subjective evaluations by country experts which are subject to biases analogous to those faced by stock analyst ratings based both on their backward-looking nature and on the herd-like behaviour of experts, scholars are increasingly turning to objective measures of the checks and balances of the political system[8] as well as of the media, financial market development and policy stability. These measures offer substantive gains on the more widely used surveys as managers are basing their behaviour not on the past outcomes realized in a country but the likely future outcomes which are based on underlying institutional structures rather than past trends that may be influenced by a host of exogenous factors unlikely to continue in the future. The gap between perceptual or subjective and these objective measures is likely to be particularly large at the peak of a bubble or at the apex of an investment cycle. This upward bias at the riskiest moments should give investors and researchers serious cause for concern.

Demand-side pressures for institutional change

In addition to these supply-side factors measuring underlying structural characteristics of a country's institutional environment, interest group theories or distributive theories of politics emphasize the demand-side determinants of policy and institutional change. One area of scrutiny is the impact of heterogeneity in the strength of interest groups defined along geographic, industry, market segment, class, racial, ethnic or religious dimensions on their ability to influence policy outcomes. The level of sophistication in this analysis varies widely including simple predictions regarding positive associations between interest group concentration, size and profitability and the incidence (Dickie, 1984; Masters and Keim, 1986; Salamon and Sigfried, 1977) and success (Esty and Caves, 1983; Rehbein and Lenway, 1994; Yoffie, 1988) of lobbying activity by organizations in the US context.

More sophisticated efforts drawing on single country case studies of policy change or large-scale econometric analysis of the determinants of armed conflict, apply expected utility theory to model the effects of interest group preferences, salience and capabilities. Researchers begin by surveying well-informed practitioners and policymakers regarding their own preferences, salience and capabilities as well as those of other relevant interest groups. Remaining groups are similarly surveyed and the information is entered into a unidimensional expected utility framework to generate predictions about the policy favoured by the median interest group. Such models have substantial intrinsic appeal and high success rates, as evidenced in published analyses of the post-Khomeni political transition in Iran (Mesquita, 1984), the Latin American debt crisis (Kugler, 1987), Italian budgetary negotiations (Beck and Mesquita, 1985), the Middle East conflict (Mesquita, 1990), the end of the Cold War (Mesquita, 1998), German monetary unification (Mesquita and Organski, 1992), the 1992 French referendum on Maastricht (Organski and Mesquita, 1993), South African electoral reform (Berman and Abdollahian, 1999), the risk of nuclear proliferation to Taiwan (Mesquita et al., 1993), the

Spratly Island conflict in the South China Sea (Wu and Mesquita, 1994), the post-crisis reforms in Korea (Root et al., 1999) and (tellingly given subsequent events) a critical appraisal of the likelihood that the 1993 accord with North Korea would substantively constrain North Korea's nuclear ambitions (Newman and Bridges, 1994). The success of these efforts, as is always the case, depends crucially on the quality of the data entered into the modelling framework. Of particular concern is the models' omission of the supply side of the policymaking process which could generate erroneous indicators of pivotal actors or decision points unless respondents are incorporating information on the policymaking structure into their survey responses.

Another line of research holds interest group characteristics constant and examines the link between the macroeconomic or social conditions faced by interest groups as a whole and the strength of lobbying for policies that insulate a given interest group from adversity. Examples include the endogenous trade policy literature (Magee et al., 1989) and the related international studies which posit a link between openness and the depth of the welfare state (Adsera and Boix, 2001; Alesina and Wacziarg, 1998; Rodrik, 1998).

Researchers in social movement theory examine the conditions under which individuals and interest groups not directly implicated in a policy debate or adversely affected by economic and social conditions may still be mobilized for the purpose of a campaign to change or defeat a proposed change in institutional structure. Key insights here include the importance of framing an issue such that relatively uninformed or apathetic parties interpret the debate with reference to better established pre-existing beliefs and biases. A prominent example from the field of international business is the invocation of national competitiveness frames by advocates in the standard-setting debate for high-definition television (Dowell et al., 2002). One of the most powerful examples of such frames is the normative principle of fairness which requires 'like treatment of like cases' (Zajac, 1995). Henisz and Zelner (2005) draw upon such frameworks in their examination of the determinants of change in the emergent institutional structures that support private sector investment in electricity generation.

Research that highlights the demand-side determinants of institutional change call attention not merely to the structure of existing institutions but the structure of the interest group coalitions that support them, the macroeconomic and social conditions that can lead to interest group support for radical policy change and the framing devices that can enhance the likelihood of such militancy for a given interest group structure and economic and social environment. Beyond scattered case studies, international business research has devoted little systematic attention to these forces and their impact on institutional change within existing and potential host countries.

Conclusion

If the defining characteristic of international business research is its cross-border nature, such research should incorporate recent findings from relevant disciplines on the nature of the institutional environment that constitutes a nation state and its impact on cross-border economic transactions. The review provided here argues that while integration has proceeded well regarding the impact of cross-sectional variation (i.e. the differences in the nature of business transactions across nations with varying institutional environments), research on time series variation (i.e. the differences in the nature of business transactions when the supply-side structure of the institutional environment or demand-side forces are likely to generate future change in that institutional environment) remains limited. Future research in the field should both draw upon and contribute to the growing body of international political economy work that speaks to the importance of national institutional environments for economic outcomes with an emphasis on the role that international business can have on the development of national institutions over time.

Notes

1. This section substantially draws upon Henisz and Delios (2002).
2. This hypothesis is strongly supported by the only available empirical study (Bradley, 1977). The author finds that expropriation of joint ventures exclusively between foreign multinationals is eight times as likely as expropriation of joint ventures that involve local partners.
3. Henisz (2000) demonstrates that this relationship is conditional upon the nature of the assets under the purview of the overseas subsidiary while Delios and Henisz (2000) argue that the strength of the linkage is inversely correlated to a firm's relevant experience.

4. See especially Krehbiel (1991) on information specialization and Kiewit and McCubbins (1991) and Cox and McCubbins (1993) on party delegation.
5. An earlier but thoughtful related treatment is provided in Berman (1983).
6. 'I am the state.'
7. See Heller (2001) for an alternate set of theoretical arguments and empirical evidence highlighting the potential in Parliamentary democracies for party discipline to dominate logrolling thus allowing for a negative relationship between bicameralism and budget deficits.
8. See, in particular, http://www-management.wharton.upenn.edu/henisz/ for the political constraints dataset and also http://www.worldbank.org/ research/bios/pkeefer.htm for the Database of Political Institutions.

References

Adsera, Alicia and Carles Boix (2001) 'Trade, Democracy and the Size of the Public Sector: the Political Underpinnings of Openness', *International Organization*, 56(2): 229–62.

Agarwal, Sanjeev and Sridhar N. Ramaswami (1992) 'Choice of Foreign Market Entry Mode: Impact of Ownership, Location and Internalization Factors', *Journal of International Business Studies*, 23(1): 1–27.

Ahn, Sanghoon and Philip Hemmings (2000) 'Policy Influences on Economic Growth in OECD Countries: an Evaluation of the Evidence', OECD Economics Working Paper, 2000(19).

Alesina, Alberto and Roman Wacziarg (1998) 'Openness, Country Size and Government', *Journal of Public Economics*, 69: 305–21.

Alt, James E. and Robert C. Lowry (1994) 'Divided Government and Budget Deficits: Evidence for the States', *American Political Science Review*, 88(4): 811–28.

Barkema, Harry G., John H. J. Bell and Johannes M. Pennings (1996) 'Foreign Entry, Cultural Barriers, and Learning', *Strategic Management Journal*, 17(2): 151–66.

Barkema, Harry G. and Freek Vermeulen (1997) 'What Differences in the Cultural Backgrounds of Partners are Detrimental for International Joint Ventures', *Journal of International Business Studies*, 28(4): 845–64.

Baron, David P. (1998) 'Comparative Dynamics of Parliamentary Governments', *American Political Science Review*, 92(3): 593–610.

Bawn, Kathleen (1999) 'Money and Majorities in the Federal Republic of Germany: Evidence for a Veto Players Model of Government Spending', *American Journal of Political Science*, 43(3): 707–36.

Beamish, Paul W. (1988) *Multinational Joint Ventures in Developing Countries*. New York: Routledge.

Beck, Douglas and Bruce Bueno de Mesquita (1985) 'Forecasting Policy Decisions: an Expected Utility Approach', in S. Andriole (ed.), *Corporate Crisis Management*, Princeton, NJ: Princeton Books.

Bekaert, Geer, Campbell Harvey and Christian Lundblad (2001) 'Does Financial Liberalization Spur Growth?' NBER Working Paper, 7763.

Bennet, Peter D. and Robert T. Green (1972) 'Political Instability as a Determinant of Direct Foreign Investment in Marketing', *Journal of Marketing Research*, 19(May): 182–6.

Bergara Duque, Mario E., Witold J. Henisz and Pablo T. Spiller (1998) 'Political Institutions and Electric Utility Investment: a Cross-nation Analysis', *California Management Review*, 40(2): 18–35.

Berman, Diane R. and Mark Andrew Abdollahian (1999) 'Negotiating the Peaceful Expansion of the South African Electorate', *Journal of Conflict Resolution*, 43(2): 229–44.

Berman, Harold Joseph (1983) *Law and Revolution: the Formation of the Western Legal Tradition*. Cambridge, Mass.: Harvard University Press.

Biggart, Nicole Woolsey and Mauro F. Guillén (1999) 'Developing Difference: Social Organization and the Rise of the Auto Industries of South Korea, Taiwan, Spain and Argentina', *American Sociological Review*, 64: 722–47.

Boix, Carles (2001) 'Democracy, Development and the Public Sector', *American Journal of Political Science*, 45.

Bottom, William, Ceryl L. Eavey, Gary J. Miller and Jennifer Nicoll Victor (2000) 'The Institutional Effect on Majority Rule Instability: Bicameralism in Spatial Policy Decisions', *American Journal of Political Science*, 44(3): 523–40.

Bradley, David (1977) 'Managing against Expropriation', *Harvard Business Review*, July–August: 75–83.

Butler, Monika and Heinz Hauser (2000) 'An Economic Analysis of the New WTO Dispute Settlement System'. Mimeo.

Caballero, Richardo J. and Mohamad L. Hammour (1998) 'The Macroeconomics of Specificity', *Journal of Political Economy*, 106(4): 724–68.

Cameron, Charles, Jeffrey Segal and Donald Songer (2000) 'Strategic Auditing in a Political Hierarchy: an Informational Model of the Supreme Court's Certiorari Decisions', *American Political Science Review*, 94(1): 101–16.

Carroll, Glenn R. and Jacques Delacroix (1982) 'Organizational Mortality in the Newspapers Industries of Argentina and Ireland', *Administrative Science Quarterly*, 27: 169–98.

Chang, Sea Jin and Jaebum Hong (2000) 'Economic Performance of Group-affiliated Companies in Korea: Intragroup Resource Sharing and Internal Business Transactions', *Academy of Management Journal*, 43(3): 429–48.

Collier, Paul and Jan Willem Gunning (1999) 'Why Has Africa Grown Slowly?', *Journal of Economic Perspectives*, 13(3): 3–22.

Cox, Gary W. and Matthew D. McCubbins (1993) *Legislative Leviathan: Party Government in the House*. Berkeley, Calif.: University of California Press.

Crain, W. Mark and Lisa K. Oakley (1995) 'The Politics of Infrastructure', *Journal of Law and Economics*, 38(April): 1–17.

Dailami, Mansoor and Danny Leipziger (1998) 'Infrastructure Project Finance and Capital Flows: a New Perspective', *World Development*, 26(7): 1283–98.

Daniels, Ron and Michael J. Trebilcock (1994) 'Private Provision of Public Infrastructure: the Next Privatization Frontier?', Paper presented at IDS-270.

Davidson, William H. and Donald G. McFetridge (1985) 'Key Characteristics in the Choice of International Technology Transfer Mode', *Journal of International Business Studies*, 16(2): 5–21.

de Figueiredo, John M. and Emerson H. Tiller (1996) 'Congressional Control of the Courts: a Theoretical and Empirical Analysis of Expansion of the Federal Judiciary', *Journal of Law and Economics*, 39(2): 435–62.

Delios, Andrew and Paul Beamish (1999) 'Ownership Strategy of Japanese Firms: Transactional, Institutional and Experience Influences', *Strategic Management Journal*, 20: 711–27.

Delios, Andrew and Witold J. Henisz (2000) 'Japanese Firms' Investment Strategies in Emerging Economies', *Academy of Management Journal*, 43(3): 305–23.

Delios, Andrew and Witold J. Henisz (2003a) 'Political Hazards and the Sequence of Entry by Japanese Firms', *Journal of International Business Studies*, 34(3): 227–41.

Delios, Andrew and Witold J. Henisz (2003b) 'Political Hazards, Experience and Sequential Entry Strategies: the International Expansion of Japanese Firms, 1980–1998', *Strategic Management Journal*, 24(12): forthcoming.

Dickie, R. (1984) 'Influence of Public Affairs Office on Corporate Planning and of Corporations on Government Policy', *Strategic Management Journal*, 5(1): 15–34.

Djankov, Simeon, Rafael La Porta, Florencio Lopez de Silanes and Andrei Shleifer (2000) 'The Regulation of Entry'. NBER Working Paper, 7892.

Dowell, Glenn, Anand Swaminathan and Jim Wade (2002) 'Pretty Pictures and Ugly Scenes: Political and Technological Maneuvers in High Definition Television', *Advances in Strategic Management*, 19: 97–134.

Dyck, Alexander and Luigi Zingales (2001) 'Why Are Private Benefits of Control So Large in Certain Countries and What Effects Does This Have on Their Financial Development?', National Bureau for Economic Research Working Paper, 8711.

Erramilli, M. Krishna (1996) 'Nationality and Subsidiary Ownership Patterns in Multinational Corporations', *Journal of International Business Studies*, 27(2): 225–48.

Esfahani, Hadi Salehi and Maria Teresa Ramirez (1999) 'Institutions, Infrastructure and Economic Growth', Mimeo.

Esty, C. and R. E. Caves (1983) 'Market Structure and Political Influence: New Data on Political Expenditures, Activity and Success', *Economic Inquiry*, 21: 24–38.

Ferejohn, John and Shipan Charles (1990) 'Congressional Influence on Bureaucracy', *Journal of Law, Economics and Organization*, 6 (Special Issue): 1–20.

Fisman, Ray and Tarun Khanna (1998) 'Facilitating Development: the Role of Business Groups', Harvard Business School Working Paper, 98(76).

Foley, C. Fritz (2001) 'The Effects of Having an American Patent: an Analysis of the Growth of U.S. Mulatinational Affiliates', Mimeo.

Frankel, Jeffrey A. and David Romer (1996) 'Trade and Growth: an Empirical Investigation', NBER Working Paper (5476).

Franzese Jr, Robert J. (1999) 'The Positive Political Economy of Public Debt: an Empirical Examination of the OECD Postwar Debt Experience', Mimeo.

Gastanaga, Victor M., Jeffrey B. Nugent and Bistra Pashamova (1998) 'Host Country Reforms and FDI Inflows: How Much Difference Do They Make?', *World Development*, 26(7): 1299–314.

Gatignon, Hubert and Erin Anderson (1988) 'The Multinational Corporation's Degree of Control over Foreign Subsidiaries: an Empirical Test of a Transaction Cost Explanation', *Journal of Law, Economics and Organization*, 4(2): 305–36.

Gely, Rafael and Pablo T. Spiller (1990) 'A Rational Choice Theory of the Supreme Court Statutory Decisions with Applications to the *State Farm* and *Grove City* Cases', *Journal of Law, Economics and Organization*, 6(2): 263–301.

Gely, Rafael and Pablo T. Spiller (1992) 'The Political Economy of Supreme Court Constitutional Decisions: the Case of Roosevelt's Court-packing Plan', *International Review of Law and Economics*, 12: 45–67.

Gilligan, Thomas, W. and Keith Krehbiel (1980) 'Collective Choice without Procedural Commitment', in Peter Ordeshook (ed.), *Models of Strategic Choice in Politics*. Ann Arbor: University of Michigan Press.

Gilligan, Thomas W., William J. Marshall and Barry R. Weingast (1989) 'Regulation and the Theory of Legislative Choice: the Interstate Commerce Act of 1887', *Journal of Law and Economics*, 32(1): 35–61.

Goodnow, James D. and James E. Hansz (1972) 'Environmental Determinants of Overseas Market Entry Strategies', *Journal of International Business Studies*, 3: 33–50.

Grandy, Christopher (1989) 'Can the Government Be Trusted to Keep its Part of a Social Contract? New Jersey and the Railways, 1825–1888', *Journal of Law, Economics and Organization*, 5(2): 249–69.

Granovetter, Mark (1995) 'Coase Revisited: the Problem of Business Groups in the Modern Economy', *Industrial and Corporate Change*, 4(1): 93–130.

Green, Robert T. and William Cunningham (1975) 'The Determinants of U.S. Foreign Investment: an Empirical Examination', *Management International Review*, 15(2–3): 113–20.

Groseclose, Tim (1994a) 'The Committee Outlier Debate – a Review and a Reexamination of the Evidence', *Public Choice*, 80(3–4): 265–73.

Groseclose, Tim (1994b) 'Testing Committee Composition Hypotheses for the U.S. Congress', *Journal of Politics*, 56(2): 440–58.

Grubert, Harry and John Mutti (1991) 'Taxes, Tariffs and Transfer Pricing in Multinational Corporate Decision Making', *Review of Economics and Statistics*, 73: 285–93.

Guillén, Mauro (1994) *Models of Management: Work Authority and Organization in Comparative Perspective*. Chicago: University of Chicago Press.

Guillén, Mauro (2000) 'Business Groups in Emerging Economies: a Resource-based View', *Academy of Management Journal*, 43(3): 362–80.

Guillén, Mauro (2001) *The Limits of Convergence: Globalization and Organizational Change in Argentina, South Korea, and Spain*. Princeton, NJ: Princeton University Press.

Hallerberg, Mark and Scott Basinger (1998) 'Internationalization and Changes in Tax Policy in OECD Countries: the Importance of Domestic Veto Players', *Comparative Political Studies*, 31(June): 321–52.

Hamilton, Gary G. and Nicole W. Biggart (1988) 'Market, Culture and Authority: a Comparative Analysis of Management and Organization in the Far East', *American Journal of Sociology*, 94 (Supplement): 52–94.

Hanson, John R. II (1999) 'Culture Shock and Direct Investment in Poor Countries', *Journal of Economic History*, 59(1): 1–16.

Harris, David, Randall Morck, Joel Slemrod and Bernard Yeung (1993) 'Income Shifting in U.S. Multinational Corporations', in A. Giovannini, G. Hubbard and J. Slemrod (eds), *Studies in International Taxation*. University of Chicago Press.

Heller, William B. (2001) 'Political Denials: the Policy Effect of Intercameral Partisan Differences in Bicameral Parliamentary Systems', *Journal of Law, Economics and Organization*, 17(1): 34–61.

Henisz, Witold Jerzy (2000) 'The Institutional Environment for Multinational Investment', *Journal of Law, Economics and Organization*, 16(2): 334–64.

Henisz, Witold Jerzy (2003) 'The Power of the Buckley and Casson Thesis: the Ability to Manage Institutional Idiosyncrasies', *Journal of International Business Studies*, 34(2): 173–84.

Henisz, Witold Jerzy (2004) 'Political Institutions and Policy Volatility', *Economics and Politics*, 16(1): 1–27.

Henisz, Witold J. and Andrew Delios (2001) 'Uncertainty, Imitation, and Plant Location: Japanese Multinational Corporations, 1990–1996', *Administrative Science Quarterly*, 46(3): 443–75.

Henisz, Witold J. and Andrew Delios (2002) 'Learning about the Institutional Environment', in Paul Ingram and Brian Silverman (eds), *The New Institutionalism in Strategic Management*. New York: JAI Press.

Henisz, Witold J. and Bennet A. Zelner (2001) 'The Institutional Environment for Telecommunications Investment', *Journal of Economics and Management Strategy*, 10(1): 123–47.

Henisz, Witold J. and Bennet A. Zelner (2002) 'Interest Groups, Institutional Structures and Electricity Investment', Mimeo.

Henisz, Witold J. and Bennet A. Zelner (2005) 'Legitimacy, Interest Group Pressures and Change in Emergent Institutions: the Case of Foreign Investors and Host Country Governments', *Academy of Management Review*, 28(4): forthcoming.

Hill, Charles W. L., Peter Hwang and W. Chan Kim (1990) 'An Eclectic Theory of the Choice of International Entry Mode', *Strategic Management Journal*, 11(2): 117–28.

Hines, James R. Jr (1998) '"Tax Sparing" and Direct Investment in Developing Countries', NBER Working Paper, 6728.

Hymer, S. (1976) *The International Operations of National Firms*. Cambridge, Mass.: MIT Press.

Khanna, Tarun (2000) 'Business Groups and Social Welfare in Emerging Markets: Existing Evidence and Unanswered Questions', *European Economic Review*, 44: 748–61.

Khanna, Tarun and Krishna Palepu (1998) 'Policy Shocks, Market Intermediaries, and Corporate Strategy: Evidence from Chile and India', *Journal of Economics and Management Strategy*, 8(2): 271–310.

Khanna, Tarun and Krishna Palepu (1999) 'The Right Way to Restructure Conglomerates in Emerging Markets', *Harvard Business Review*, July–August: 125–34.

Khanna, Tarun and Krishna Palepu (2000a) 'Emerging Market Business Groups, Foreign Investors, and Corporate Governance', in National Bureau of Economic Research (ed.), *Concentrated Ownership*. Chicago: University of Chicago.

Khanna, Tarun and Krishna Palepu (2000b) 'The Future of Business Groups in Emerging Markets: Long-run Evidence from Chile', *Academy of Management Journal*, 43(3): 268–85.

Khanna, Tarun and Krishna Palepu (2000c) 'Is Group Affiliation Profitable in Emerging Markets? An Analysis of Diversified Indian Business Groups', *Journal of Finance*, 55(2): 867–91.

Khanna, Tarun and Jan W. Rivkin (2000) 'Ties that Bind Business Groups: Evidence from an Emerging Economy', Harvard Business School Division of Research Working Paper, 00(068).

Kiewiet, D. Roderick and Matthew D. McCubbins (1991) *The Logic of Delegation: Congressional Parties and the Appropriations Process*. Chicago, Ill.: University of Chicago Press.

Kogut, Bruce and Harbir Singh (1988) 'The Effect of National Culture on the Choice of Entry Mode', *Journal of International Business Studies*, 19(3): 411–32.

Krehbiel, Keith (1991) *Information and Legislative Organization*. Ann Arbor, Mich.: University of Michigan Press.

Kreppel, Amie (2000) 'Procedure and Influence: an Empirical Analysis of EP Influence under the Codecision and Cooperation Procedures', Mimeo.

Kugler, Jacek (1987) 'The Politics of Foreign Debt in Latin America: a Study of the Debtors' Cartel', *International Interactions*, 13(2): 115–44.

La Porta, Rafael, Florencio Lopez-De-Silanes, Andrei Shleifer and Robert W. Vishny (1998) 'Law and Finance', *Journal of Political Economy*, 106(6): 1113–55.

La Porta, Rafael, Florencio Lopez-De-Silanes, Andrei Shleifer and Robert W. Vishny (1999) 'Investor Protection: Origins, Consequences, Reform', NBER Working Paper, 7248.

Lee, Jeong-Yeon and Edwin Mansfield (1996) 'Intellectual Property Protection and U.S. Foreign Direct Investment', *Review of Economics and Statistics*, 78(2): 181–6.

Levine, Ross, Norman Loayza and Thorsten Beck (2000) 'Financial Intermediation and Growth: Causality and Causes', *Journal of Monetary Economics*, 46(1): 31–77.

Levine, Ross and Sara Zervos (1998) 'Stock Markets, Banks and Economic Growth', *American Economic Review*, 88(3): 537–58.

Levy, Brian and Pablo T. Spiller (1994) 'The Institutional Foundations of Regulatory, Commitment: a Comparative Analysis of Telecommunications Regulation', *Journal of Law, Economics and Organization*, 10(2): 201–46.

Levy, Brian and Pablo T. Spiller (1996) *Regulations, Institutions and Commitment*. Cambridge: Cambridge University Press.

Li, Jiatao and Stephen Guisinger (1991) 'Comparative Business Failures of Foreign-controlled Firms in the U.S.', *Journal of International Business Studies*, 22(2): 209–24.

Loree, David W. and Stephen E. Guisinger (1995) 'Policy and Non-policy Determinants of U.S. Equity Foreign Direct Investment', *Journal of International Business Studies*, 26(2): 281–99.

McNollGast (1987) 'Administrative Procedures as Instruments of Political Control', *Journal of Law, Economics and Organization*, 3(2): 243–77.

McNollGast (1989) 'Structure and Process, Politics and Policy: Administrative Arrangements and the Political Control of Agencies', *Virginia Law Review*, 75: 431–82.

Magee, Stephen P., William A. Brock and Leslie Young (1989) *Black Hole Tariffs and Endogenous Policy Theory*. New York: Cambridge University Press.

Martin, Xavier, Anand Swaminathan and Will Mitchell (1998) 'Organizational Evolution in the Interorganizational Environment: Incentives and Constraints on International Expansion Strategy', *Administrative Science Quarterly*, 43(September): 566–601.

Masters, M. S. and G. Keim (1986) 'Variation in Corporate PAC and Lobbying Activity: an Organizational and Environmental Analysis', in J. E. Post (ed.), *Research in Corporate Social Performance and Policy*. Greenwich, Conn.: JAI Press.

Mauro, Paolo (1997) 'Why Worry about Corruption?', *IMF Economic Issues*, 6.

Mesquita, Bruce Bueno de (1984) 'Forecasting Policy Decisions: an Expected Utility Approach to Post-Khomeini Iran', *PS*, 17: 226–36.

Mesquita, Bruce Bueno de (1990) 'Multilateral Negotiations: a Spatial Analysis of the Arab–Israeli Dispute', *International Organization*, 44(3): 317–40.

Mesquita, Bruce Bueno de (1998) 'The End of the Cold War: Predicting an Emergent Property', *Journal of Conflict Resolution*, 42(2): 131–55.

Mesquita, Bruce Bueno de, James Morrow and Samuel Wu (1993) 'Modeling the Risks of Nuclear Proliferation: Taiwan as an Illustration of the Method', *Security Studies* Spring/Summer: 311–31.

Mesquita, Bruce Bueno de and A. F. K. Organski (1992) 'A Mark in Time Saves Nein', *International Political Science Review*, 13(1): 81–100.

Moe, Terry and Michael Caldwell (1994) 'The Institutional Foundations of Democratic Government: a Comparison of Presidential and Parliamentary Systems', *Journal of Institutional and Theoretical Economics*, 150(1): 171–95.

Mueller, Bernardo and Carlos Pareira (1999) 'Testing Theories of Congressional Committee's Composition and Power: the Case of the Brazilian Congress', Mimeo.

Nee, Victor (1992) 'Organizational Dynamics of Market Transition: Hybrid Forms, Property Rights and Mixed Economy in China', *Administative Science Quarterly*, 33: 194–210.

Nelson, Michael A. and Ram D. Singh (1998) 'Democracy, Economic Freedom, Fiscal Policy and Growth in LDCs: a Fresh Look', *Economic Development and Cultural Change*, 46(4): 677–96.

Newman, David and Brian Bridges (1994) 'North Korean Nuclear Weapons Policy: an Expected Utility Study', *Pacific Studies*, 9(2): 61–80.

North, Douglass C. and Barry R. Weingast (1989) 'Constitutions and Commitment: the Evolution of Institutions Governing Public Choice in Seventeenth Century England', *Journal of Economic History*, 49(4): 803–32.

Organski, A. F. K. and Bruce Bueno de Mesquita (1993) 'Forecasting the 1992 French Referendum', in Roger Morgan, Jochen Lorentzen and Anna Leander (eds), *New Diplomacy in the Post-Cold War World*. New York: St. Martin's Press.

Oxley, Joanne Elizabeth (1999) 'Institutional Environment and the Mechanisms of Governance: the Impact of Intellectual Property Protection on the Structure of Inter-firm Alliances', *Journal of Economic Behavior and Organization*, 38(3): 283–310.

Palmer, Matthew (1995) 'Toward an Economics of Comparative Political Organization: Examining Ministerial Responsibility', *Journal of Law, Economics and Organization*, 11(1): 164–88.

Persson, Torsten (2001) 'Do Political Institutions Shape Economic Policy?', NBER Working Paper Series, 8214.

Persson, Torsten and Guido Tabellini (1999) 'Political Economics and Public Finance', National Bureau for Economic Research Working Paper, 7097.

Pindyck, Robert S. (1991) 'Irreversibility, Uncertainty and Investment', *Journal of Economic Literature*, 29(September): 1110–48.

Porter, Michael E. (1998) 'Clusters and the New Economics of Competition', *Harvard Business Review*, November–December: 77–90.

Porter, Michael E. (2000) 'Location, Competition and Economic Development: Local Clusters in a Global Economy', *Economic Development Quarterly*, 14(1): 15–34.

Poterba, James (1994) 'State Responses to Fiscal Crises: "Natural Experiments" for Studying the Effects of Budgetary Institutions', *Journal of Political Economy*, 102(4): 799–821.

Rajan, Raghuram G. and Luigi Zingales (1998) 'Financial Dependence and Growth', *American Economic Review*, 88(3): 559–86.

Ramamurti, Ravi (ed.) (1996) *Privatizing Monopolies: Lessons from the Telecommunications and Transport Sectors in Latin America*. Baltimore: Johns Hopkins University Press.

Ramseyer, J. Mark and Eric B. Rasmusen (2001) 'Why are Japanese Judges So Conservative in Politically Charged Cases?', *American Political Science Review*, 95(2): 331–44.

Rehbein, Kathleen and Stefanie Lenway (1994) 'Determining an Industry's Political Effectiveness with the U.S. International Trade Commission', *Business and Society*, 33(3): 270–92.

Richards, John E. (1999) 'Towards a Positive Theory of International Institutions: Regulating International Aviation Markets', *International Organization*, 53(1): 1–37.

Riker, William H. (1980) 'Implications from the Disequilibrium of Majority Rule for the Study of Institutions', *American Political Science Review*, 74(2): 432–47.

Rodrik, Dani (1998) 'Why Do More Open Economies Have Bigger Governments?', *Journal of Political Economy*, 106(5): 997–1032.

Roller, Lars-Hendrik and Leonard Waverman (2001) 'Telecommunications Infrastructure and Economic Development: a Simultaneous Approach', *American Economics Review*, 91(4): 909–23.

Root, Franklin R. and Ahmed A. Ahmed (1978) 'The Influence of Policy Instruments on Manufacturing Direct Foreign Investment in Developing Countries', *Journal of International Business Studies*, 9: 81–93.

Root, Hilton, Mark Abdollahian, Greg Beier and Jacek Kugler (1999) 'The New Korea', *Milken Institute Policy Brief*. Santa Monica, Calif.: The Milken Institute.

Roubini, Noriel and Jeffrey Sachs (1989) 'Political and Economic Determinants of Budget Deficits in the Industrial Democracies', *European Economic Review*, 33: 903–37.

Sachs, Jeffrey and Andrew Warner (1995) 'Economic Convergence and Economic Policies', National Bureau for Economic Research Working Paper, 5039.

Salamon, Lester M. and John J. Sigfried (1977) 'Economic Power and Political Influence: the Impact of Industry Structure on Public Policy', *American Political Science Review*, 71: 1026–43.

Savedoff, William and Pablo Spiller (1997) 'Commitment and Governance in Infrastructure Sectors', Manuscript prepared for an IDB Conference on Private Investment, Infrastructure Reform and Governance in Latin America and the Caribbean, 15–16 September 1997.

Schwartz, Edward P., Pablo T. Spiller and Santiago Urbiztondo (1994) 'A Positive Theory of Legislative Intent', *Law and Contemporary Problems*, 57(1): 51–74.

Shepsle, Kenneth (1986) 'Institutional Equilibrium and Equilibrium Institutions', in Herbert Weisburg (ed.), *Political Science: the Science of Politics*. New York: Agathon Press.

Shepsle, Kenneth and Barry, R. Weingast (1987) 'The Institutional Foundations of Committee Power', *American Political Science Review*, 81(1): 85–104.

Siegel, Jordan (2002) 'Can Foreign Firms Bond Themselves Effectively by Renting U.S. Securities Laws', Mimeo.

Siegel, Jordan (2003) 'Political Connectedness and the Formation of Cross-Border Alliances: a Study of Korean Firms and their American, Japanese, and European Partners (1987–2000)', Mimeo.

Smarzynska, Beata K. and Shang-Jin Wei (2000) 'Corruption and Composition of Foreign Direct Investment: Firm-level Evidence', Mimeo, The World Bank.

Songer, Donald R., Charles M. Cameron, and Jeffrey A. Segal (1995) 'An Empirical Test of the Rational-actor Theory of Litigation', *Journal of Politics*, 57(4): 119–30.

Songer, Donald R., Jeffrey A. Segal, and Charles M. Cameron (1994) 'The Hierarchy of Justice: Testing a Principal–Agent Model of Supreme Court–Circuit Court Interactions', *American Journal of Political Science*, 38(3): 673–96.

Spiller, Pablo T. (1990) 'Politicians, Interest Groups, and Regulators: a Multiple-Principals Agency Theory of Regulation, or "Let Them Be Bribed"', *Journal of Law and Economics*, 33(1): 65–101.

Spiller, Pablo T. (1992) 'Agency Discretion under Judicial Review', *Mathematical Computer Modeling*, 16(8–9): 185–200.

Spiller, Pablo T. and Rafael Gely (1992) 'Congressional Control or Judicial Independence: the Determinants of U.S. Supreme Court Labor-relations Decisions, 1949–1988', *RAND Journal of Economics*, 23(4): 463–92.

Spiller, Pablo T. and Emerson H. Tiller (1996) 'Invitations to Override: Congressional Reversals of Supreme Court Decisions', *International Review of Law and Economics*, 16(4): 503–21.

Spiller, Pablo T. and Emerson H. Tiller (1997) 'Decision Costs and Strategic Design of Administrative Process and Judicial Review', *The Journal of Legal Studies*, 26(2 (part 1)): 347–70.

Spiller, Pablo T. and Ingo Vogelsang (1996) 'The Institutional Foundations of Regulatory Commitment in the UK (with Special Emphasis on Telecommunication)', in Brian Levy and Pablo Spiller (eds), *Regulations, Institutions and Commitment*. Cambridge University Press.

Stobaugh, Robert (1969) 'How to Analyze Foreign Investment Climates', *Harvard Business Review*, September–October: 100–8.

Tanzi, Vito and Hamid Davoddi (1997) 'Corruption, Public Investment and Growth', IMF Working Paper 97/139.

Treisman, Daniel (2000) 'Decentralization and Inflation: Commitment, Collective Action or Continuity', *American Political Science Review*, 94(4): 837–57.

Tsebelis, George (1995) 'Decision-making in Political Systems: Veto Players in Presidentialism, Parliamentarism, Multicameralism and Multipartyism', *British Journal of Political Science*, 25(3): 289–325.

Tsebelis, George and Geoffrey Garrett (2000) 'The Institutional Foundations of Intergovernmentalism and Supranationalism in the European Union', *International Organization*, 55(2): 357–90.

Vernon, Raymond (1977) 'The Strain on National Objectives: the Developing Countries', in *Storm over the Multinationals: the Real Issues*. Cambridge, Mass.: Harvard University.

Wei, Shang-Jin (2000) 'How Taxing Is Corruption on International Investors?', *Review of Economics and Statistics*, 82(1): 1–11.

Weingast, Barry N. (1981) 'Regulation, Reregulation and Deregulation: the Political Foundations of Agency Clientele Relationships', *Law and Contemporary Problems*, 44(1): 149–77.

Weingast, Barry (1984) 'The Congressional Bureaucratic System: a Principal–agent Perspective (with Applications to the SEC)', *Public Choice*, 44(1): 147–91.

Weingast, Barry (1993) 'Constitutions as Governance Structures: the Political Foundations of Secure Markets', *Journal of Institutional and Theoretical Economics*, 149(1 (March)): 286–311.

Weingast, Barry and William J. Marshall (1988) 'The Industrial Organization of Congress; or, Why Legislators, like Firms, are not Organized as Markets', *Journal of Political Economy*, 96(1): 132–63.

Weingast, Barry and Mark Moran (1983) 'Bureaucratic Discretion or Congressional Control? Regulatory Policymaking by the Federal Trade Commission', *Journal of Political Economy*, 91(5): 765–800.

Williamson, Oliver E. (1976) 'Franchise Bidding with Respect to CATV and in General', *Bell Journal of Economics*, Spring: 73–104.

Wu, Samuel and Bruce Bueno de Mesquita (1994) 'Assessing the Dispute in the South China Sea: a Model of China's Security Decision Making', *International Studies Quarterly*, 38: 379–403.

Yoffie, David B. (1988) 'How an Industry Builds Political Advantage', *Harvard Business Review*, May–June: 82–9.

Zaheer, Srilata (1995) 'Overcoming the Liability of Foreignness', *Academy of Management Journal*, 38(2): 341–63.

Zaheer, Srilata and Elaine Mosakowski (1997) 'The Dynamics of the Liability of Foreignness: a Global Study of Survival in Financial Services', *Strategic Management Journal*, 18(6): 439–64.

Zajac, Edward E. (1995) *Political Economy of Fairness*. Cambridge, Mass.: MIT Press.

7
Regional Multinationals: the New Research Agenda

Alan M. Rugman and Alain Verbeke

Introduction

One of the puzzles of international business research is that the key actor, the multinational enterprise (MNE), appears to have a very unevenly distributed geographic dispersion of sales. The MNE is usually a regionalized rather than a globalized business. Three definitions matter:

1. Multinational enterprise: a firm with operations across national borders;
2. Global business: a firm with major operations (at least 20 per cent of its total sales) in each of the three broad regions of the 'broad triad' of the European Union (EU), North America and Asia;
3. Regional business: a firm with the majority of its sales inside one of the triad regions, usually the home region.

Given these definitions the following empirical observations can be made:

1. The world's 500 largest MNEs account for over 90 per cent of the world's stock of foreign direct investment (FDI) and over half of world trade, usually in the form of intra-firm sales;
2. Of these 500 MNEs, only nine are 'global' in the sense of having a substantial presence (at least 20 per cent of sales) in each region of the triad;
3. The vast majority of the 500 MNEs (320 of the 380 for which data are available) have an average of 80 per cent of their sales in their home region of the broad triad.

These stylized facts suggest a new research agenda for the international business field, as requested by Buckley (2002). In this essay, we explore some aspects of this. The observed regionalization can be given a simple transaction cost economics (TCE) explanation. Host regions require substantial 'linking' or 'melding' investments (a form of asset specificity), in order to integrate the MNE's existing firm-specific advantages (FSAs) and exogenous country-specific advantages (CSAs), whereas such investments, driven by cultural, administrative, geographic and economic distance, are much lower in the home region. This perspective on international business leads to a new 'big question' for the field: why are we still teaching global business when much of it is actually regional?

Empirical evidence on regionalization

For the 365 firms included in our study of the world's largest 500 firms, data were available that permitted a regional decomposition of their foreign sales. It should be noted that many of the remaining 134 companies are actually operating solely in their home region, with no sales elsewhere, and for some others there are insufficient data. Of the 366 with data, the vast majority (320) is home-triad region based, having few sales in the other two parts of the triad. A limited set is 'bi-regional', which we define as having at least 20 per cent of sales in two legs of the triad. Only nine MNEs are truly 'global', with at least 20 per cent of their sales in all three parts of the triad. This picture of regionalization, rather than globalization, is shown in Table 7.1. These data and their implications are discussed in more detail in Rugman and Verbeke (2004). The MNEs included were ranked in descending order according to sales, with Wal-Mart currently being the world's largest company.

The definitions adopted in Table 7.1 are as follows:

(a) Home-triad region oriented: 320 firms have at least 50 per cent of their sales in their home region of the triad. The threshold of 50 per cent was chosen as we assume that a region representing more than 50 per cent of total sales will systematically both shape and constrain the most important decisions and actions taken by the MNE. It also implies comparatively inexpensive (vis-à-vis what would be required in host regions) linking investments between its FSAs and

Table 7.1   Classification of the top 500 MNEs

Type of MNE	No. of MNEs	% of 500	% of 380	Weighted average % of intra-regional sales
Global	9	2.0	2.6	38.3
Bi-regional	25	5.0	6.6	42.0
Host region oriented	11	2.2	2.9	30.9
Home region oriented	320	64.0	84.2	80.3
Insufficient data	15	2.8	3.7	40.9
No data	120	24.0		NA
Total	**500**	**100.0**	**100.0**	

Note: Data are for 2001, based on calculations by the authors from the largest 500 firms.
Source: Braintrust Research Group: The Regional Nature of Global Multinational Activity, 2003.

location advantages in that region. In fact, following Porter (1990) and Rugman and Verbeke (1995), it could be argued that FSAs to some extent grow out of CSAs in the home location, or at least that linkages between FSAs and location advantages are easy to establish in the home region sphere.

(b) Bi-regional: 25 MNEs are bi-regional, defined as firms with at least 20 per cent of their sales in each of two regions, but less than 50 per cent in any one region. This set includes 25 firms with sales ranging between 20 and 50 per cent in the home region and 20 per cent or over in a second region. The threshold of 20 per cent was chosen because we assume that having two regional markets each representing at least one-fifth of a '$10+billion' firm's sales reflects impressive market success resulting from extensive linkages between FSAs at the customer end, and location advantages in those two markets. The question could then be raised whether a particular absolute volume of sales, irrespective of the 20 per cent threshold percentage, would make a firm bi-regional. In our framework, an absolute sales volume is, in itself, insufficient. We view the status of a region from a micro-level, corporate-strategy perspective; here, this status is fully dependent on the relative sales achieved vis-à-vis market performance in other regions.

(c) Host-triad region oriented: 11 firms have more than 50 per cent of their sales in a triad market other than the home-triad region.

(d) Global: only nine of the MNEs included are global, defined as having sales of 20 per cent or more in each of the three parts of the triad; the 20 per cent figure is less than the one-third required for an equal triad distribution, and so is biased downwards in favour of finding global MNEs. Conceptually, it implies the successful establishment of linkages between customer-end FSAs and market-related location advantages in three distinct markets. The North American and European region of the broad triad are of approximate equal size, as measured by GDP. Asia is smaller than either, as measured by GDP, but is nearly equal when adjusting the data in order to respect purchasing power parity (PPP). In other words, giving weights to each of the three broad triad regions according to GDP, with or without corrections for PPP, will not generate more global firms.

Within each of the groups above, the home-triad region sales weighted averages are as follows:

(a) Home-triad region oriented (320 firms): 80.3 per cent
(b) Bi-regional (25 firms): 42 per cent
(c) Host-triad region oriented (11 firms): 30.9 per cent
(d) Global (9 firms): 38.3 per cent

Of the 380 companies for which data can be classified by percentiles, 58 are purely home-triad region based (15.3 per cent of the total). Another 69 have over 90 per cent or more of their sales in the home region (18.2 per cent), and a total of 230 have over 70 per cent or more of their sales in their home-triad region. Those with over 50 per cent or more intra-regional sales add up to the 320 identified above as home-triad region based. This reflects an extraordinary degree of regionalization, rather than globalization. These data also confirm the study of the 49 retail MNEs in the 500 (Rugman and Girod, 2003). In that study, only one retail MNE was found to be global, namely LVMH (Moët Hennessy Louis Vuitton SA).

Further research should be undertaken to test for the regional dimension of international strategy. Specifically, key analytical devices used in international business research will need to be modified. For example, the economic integration–national responsiveness matrix popularized by Bartlett and Ghoshal (1989) needs to be complemented with a regional dimension, as discussed below.

One of the clearest examples of regionalization is the automobile industry. This industry is characterized by triad-based clusters with regionally situated MNEs. The data on foreign sales of the world's largest automobile MNEs show that sales, as well as assembly and production, are regional (Rugman, 2000). GM has 81 per cent of its sales in North America; Ford has 61 per cent; BMW and VW have the majority of their sales in Europe. DaimlerChrysler, Nissan Motors, Honda and Toyota are bi-regional. None of these firms is global.

In terms of the value chain, a number of MNEs source offshore. Nike has 99 per cent of its production outside of the United States, almost all of this in South-East Asia. This type of globalization, at the upstream end of the value chain, is easier to achieve than at the customer end, because the linking investments required to meld the MNE's key FSAs (brand names and logistics skills) with location advantages in production do not, in this case at least, require high location-specific adaptation investments to tap into the foreign-location advantages.

The service sectors are even more local and regional than is manufacturing. In retail, only one of the largest 49 retail firms is global (LVMH), and only two are bi-regional (Rugman and Girod, 2003). In banking, all the companies have the vast majority of their assets in the home region.

Despite Levitt's (1983) prediction of standardization through globalization, and of global brands, there is no discernible trend towards either standardization or global branding. Indeed, banks remain stubbornly local or regional. Only a few MNEs, with Coca-Cola leading the way, are global. Even McDonald's is bi-regional not global. In marketing, research shows that location-driven adaptation costs are incurred, in order to be successful. There is little evidence of an increased commonality in demand for products and services. Even successful MNEs, with internationally recognized brands, need to allocate substantial resources to craft linkages between their FSAs and foreign-location advantages, in order to outperform local rivals.

Health care is not a global business, as it is delivered locally and is subject to local regulations. Even within the EU, there are separate national systems for health care delivery and for pharmaceuticals. Within NAFTA, there are three distinct health care systems, so health care is not even regional, let alone global. Patents are registered at the national level; the most active is the US patent office where all active MNEs attempt to register.

Implications for MNE theory

Conventional international business theory suggests that international sales arise because firms possess firm-specific advantages (FSAs), i.e. proprietary knowledge, which can be exploited profitably across national borders, whether through exports, foreign direct investment, market contracts or hybrid modes. Further, and especially in the context of market-seeking investment, internalization advantages, in the sense of comparatively higher efficiency of hierarchy vis-à-vis other entry modes, are critical to the explanation of FDI and the establishment of foreign subsidiaries. Finally, location advantages or country-specific advantages (CSAs), are important in explaining the precise geographic scope of international expansion (Dunning, 1993; Rugman, 1981, 1996). Given the above, the regional concentration of sales of the world's 500 largest MNEs is puzzling. Why would most American, European and Asian MNEs in a single industry have a concentration of their sales in their home region, if they (a) possess proprietary knowledge that is internationally transferable/exploitable, (b) can benefit from similar internalization advantages associated with FDI, building upon this proprietary knowledge, and (c) most importantly, face similar location advantages critical to successful market-seeking investment?

One, albeit unsatisfactory, explanation is provided by internationalization theory (Johansson and Vahlne, 1977, 1990). This theory argues that MNEs expand first in geographically proximate markets and engage in modest resource commitments. As experiential learning is built up, firms venture into more distant markets and engage in more complex and more far-reaching resource commitments. The problem with internationalization theory is that it lacks serious conceptual grounding and generalizability, especially as regards what exactly constitutes geographic proximity or experiential learning, and the mechanisms through which these concepts influence FDI decisions and geographic sales dispersion.

A more useful explanation of regional MNE activity, fully in line with the modern TCE theory of the firm, is that the scope of geographic expansion is determined by the MNE's ability to link its FSAs with location advantages abroad. International success does not simply follow from proprietary knowledge in, for example, R&D or marketing, but from the MNE's ability to adapt successfully the deployment of its existing FSAs to the specific circumstances of foreign markets, i.e. by better aligning FSAs and CSAs. We have argued elsewhere (Rugman and Verbeke, 1992, 2001, 2003c, 2004) that such adaptation can take several forms, especially (a) investments in the development of location-bound FSAs in foreign markets (leading to benefits of national responsiveness) to complement non-location-bound FSAs, and (b) investments in the development of new, non-location-bound FSAs in foreign subsidiaries.

It could be argued that there is nothing new in this analysis; MNEs are faced with the liability of foreignness, i.e. additional costs of doing business abroad, and such costs are simply higher in host-region markets than in home-region markets. However, our proposition is that, at the market side, these costs could be viewed as the result of implicit contracts with foreign locations, whereby the intended outcome is stronger embeddedness of the firm's extended knowledge base in these foreign locations, and therefore higher sales. In other words, asset specificity (in the form of additional, location-specific linking investments) is incurred, implying that such transactions, even if successful, come at a cost, as compared to the conventional deployment of FSAs in locations where no such linking investments need to be made to increase sales.

This problem is compounded by the fact that the MNE's commitment of resources to link its existing pool of FSAs with foreign-location advantages (such as the presence of a large market), through crafting location-bound FSAs or even new, non-location-bound FSAs in foreign markets, in no way guarantees success. The resource commitments made to attract potential foreign customers and to increase sales are fully one-sided. This is in contrast with, for example, resource-seeking or strategic asset-seeking FDI, whereby foreign locations may again require location-specific linking investments from the MNE, but whereby all relevant parties, such as foreign suppliers, workers, and acquired companies themselves engage in reciprocal commitments to make these investments worthwhile.

The above analysis suggests that the puzzle of regional concentration of sales has transaction cost-related origins: in the case of market-driven geographic expansion, what is conventionally viewed as the MNE's proprietary knowledge (its FSAs), is not just deployed in geographic space in those locations where exogenously determined CSAs (in this case an attractive market) are the greatest in an objective sense. Each foreign location requires location-specific linking investments to meld existing FSAs with CSAs, and it is, *ceteris paribus*, the extent of these adaptation costs, taking into account the redeployability of the resulting additional knowledge in the relevant locations, that explains why most MNEs expand first in their home region, and may face great difficulty expanding to other regions.

More specifically, many so-called non-location-bound FSAs can only be exploited profitably within the home region, without the need for substantial, location-specific adaptation investments. In addition, location-bound FSAs developed in the home country or in other countries in the home region can be 'tuned up' to be fully deployable in the entire region, with low linking investments required, if the countries involved are subject to a low cultural, administrative, geographic and economic distance among themselves, in the spirit of Ghemawat (2001). Hence, these FSAs can easily be made 'region-bound', to the extent that linking investments with high cultural specificity, administrative specificity, geography-related specificity and economy-related specificity can be avoided. This process is further enhanced if governments in this region pursue policies that promote internal coherence via administrative and political harmonization (as in the EU) or even merely via economic integration (as in NAFTA and Asia), thereby reducing the MNE's needs to engage in idiosyncratic, location-specific adaptation investments to meld existing FSAs and foreign-location advantages. In contrast, host regions may require large adaptation investments driven by home/host region differences in the cultural, administrative, geographic and economic sphere in order to meld the MNE's existing knowledge base and the host-region location advantages. This requirement for high, region-specific 'linking' investments acts as an entry deterrent for many MNEs.

A related point is that inter-block business is likely to be restricted relative to intra-regional sales by government imposed barriers to entry. For example, the EU and the United States are likely to fight trade wars and be responsive to domestic business lobbies seeking shelter in the form of subsidies and/or protection. Cultural, administrative, geography-related and economy-related differences among members of a single triad region may remain, but these will mostly be less significant than across triad regions (Rugman, 2000). The end result is the persistence of MNEs that will continue to earn 80 per cent or more of their income in their home-triad region. There will only be a limited number of purely 'global' MNEs in the top 500.

In contrast, as mentioned above, transactions that do not relate to sales (or the customer end of the value chain) but to more upstream activities, are not one-sided (meaning the MNE engages in location-specific adaptation investments without any customer guarantees to purchase the MNEs products). Upstream value-chain activities entail transactions whereby all relevant economic actors may make credible commitments to craft a highly efficient manufacturing or logistics chain apparatus (including workers, outside component suppliers, logistics providers, etc.).

Regionalization and the integration/national responsiveness framework

Perhaps the most important implications of the empirical data on triad-based MNE activities are for research adopting a resource-based approach to MNE functioning. The integration/national responsiveness framework developed by Bartlett and Ghoshal (1989) was given a resource-based interpretation by Rugman and Verbeke (1992). The latter authors have argued that benefits of integration, in the form of scale economies, scope economies, and benefits of exploiting national differences, require non-location-bound FSAs. In contrast, benefits of national responsiveness require location-bound FSAs. The data presented in this chapter, however, suggest the need for a radical extension of the framework, as suggested in Figure 7.1(a, b, c).

Figure 7.1(a) provides a stylized, alternative representation of the conventional integration/national responsiveness framework. Here, the horizontal axis describes the discrete set of critical activities (elements of the various value-chain functions) to be performed by MNEs in order to be successful in foreign markets in terms of effectively selling a particular product in those foreign markets. The tasks, numbered from 1 to n, are arranged as a function of the relative needs for non-location-bound FSAs (area NLB) and location-bound FSAs (area LB), with an increasing need for the latter. Bartlett and Ghoshal's (1989) 'transnational solution' case can then simply be interpreted as a firm that can effectively access and deploy the required dual knowledge bundles (of NLB and LB areas) for each activity to be performed, for each product, within each strategic

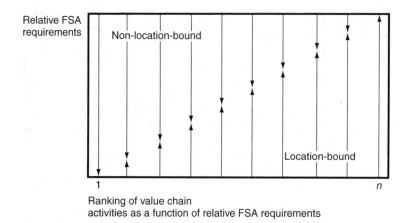

Figure 7.1(a) A resource-based reinterpretation of the integration–responsiveness framework

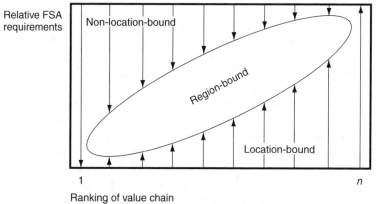

Figure 7.1(b) A conceptual extension of the resource-based integration–responsiveness framework: the home-region case

business unit. Here, the location-bound FSAs typically result from the linking investments mentioned above (they are the 'glue' that melds the MNE's non-location-bound FSAs and the CSAs). In addition, each 'generic' subsidiary type (namely strategic leaders, contributors, implementers and black holes), receives access to an idiosyncratic set of

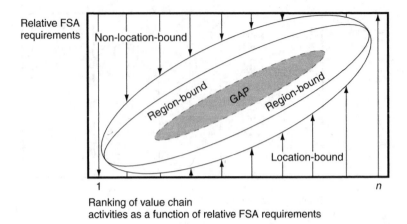

Figure 7.1(c) A conceptual extension of the resource-based integration–responsiveness framework: the host-region case

FSA bundles or resources to create such bundles, thereby guaranteeing appropriate selectivity in resource allocation. The basic framework described in Figure 7.1(a) does not take into account the learning imperative, the resource-based implications which have been discussed elsewhere; see Rugman and Verbeke (2001).

The conventional framework needs to be augmented since operating in the *home*-triad region may be associated with new needs for the development of *region-bound* FSAs, i.e. new linking investments, imposed by regional integration; see, for example, the nine cases discussed by Rugman and Verbeke (1991), especially the Volvo Trucks case. Region-bound FSAs reflect the successful creation of linkages between, on the one hand, a firm's initial set of location-bound and non-location-bound FSAs, and, on the other hand, the location advantages of the regional market where it operates. This situation is represented in Figure 7.1(b), where many activities require a set of region-bound FSAs. Hence, regional integration creates both a threat and an opportunity for MNEs as they need to complement the conventional bundles of non-location-bound FSAs and location-bound FSAs with a set of additional, region-bound FSAs. The data in this chapter suggest that many of the world's largest and most international MNEs have been quite successful in doing so.

In contrast, for the case of MNEs in *host*-triad regions, few of these firms have been capable of developing and deploying the required set of region-bound FSAs, supposed to link a firm's initial FSA bundle with the location advantages of the host region. Instead, a too limited set of region-bound FSAs is usually created, leading to a competence gap. This is represented by the area within the dotted lines in Figure 7.1(c). Here, the decay of the non-location-bound FSAs (in the sense of misalignment with the host-region location advantages) occurs at a much faster rate (depending upon the differences between the regions involved) than in the home-triad region. This is compounded by the fact that region-bound FSAs cannot be simply created at a low cost to fill the competence gap. This is in contrast with the home-triad leg case, whereby the reach of conventional location-bound FSAs is extended across borders, or non-location-bound FSAs are 'regionally sharpened', at a low cost, and a competence gap can be avoided. This explains why many MNE operations in host regions are primarily sensing instruments with little real effectiveness in market terms, thus giving these operations a 'black hole' status.

In this context of two generic FSA types, it is interesting to observe, as noted in the previous section, that many large MNEs are much less home-region based in their sourcing than in their sales, both in resource industries and manufacturing, but appear incapable of capitalizing on this broader geographical sourcing to achieve global sales penetration. This has two critical implications. First, it means that the concept of location-bound versus non-location-bound FSAs needs to be extended. The former concept usually implies that profitable deployment is possible only in the home country. It is therefore unlikely that location-specific linking investments in foreign nations would permit the crafting of successful linkages between the MNE's FSA base, and the foreign-location advantages. The latter concept assumes global transferability, which implies a relative ease in successfully linking the firm's FSA base with foreign-location advantages.

The data suggest that many MNEs have developed FSAs that are home-region bound, as a result of linking successfully the MNE's initial FSA base with the location advantages characteristic of this home region. Here, value added through aggregation, in the sense of exploiting similarities across countries (Ghemawat, 2003), can be achieved in the home region but appears difficult across regions. Second, the requirement of linking the MNE's initial FSA base with location advantages abroad, appears easier to satisfy in more upstream activities, thereby leading to broad geographic sourcing (of R&D outputs, raw materials, intermediate inputs, labour and capital) and production. Here, value added through arbitrage (Ghemawat, 2003), i.e. successfully linking the firm's FSA base with a sequence of location advantages arising in a variety of foreign countries, appears to be achievable more often across regions.

Implications of regionalization for business strategy

In this chapter, globalization is defined in terms of geographic dispersion of sales across regions, with regional effects being potentially very different in upstream and customer-end activities, given the differential ease to develop linkages between the firm's FSA base and the relevant location advantages at the upstream versus customer end. For example, some firms, such as Nike and Wal-Mart, have sourcing structures that may be much more geographically dispersed than their sales. Global sourcing of primary and intermediate inputs, as well as dispersed production, may greatly contribute to a firm's success in its home region. However, ultimately it is market penetration (if achieved in a profitable way) that provides the best, in fact the only, indicator of global corporate success. What are the immediate managerial implications of the observed geographic concentration of sales in most MNEs, beyond the broader research issues discussed above? The following five managerial implications are critical.

First, the regional issues discussed in this chapter, whether viewed as opportunities or threats, cast additional doubts on the validity of the transnational solution model as the panacea for global corporate success. The main weakness of the transnational solution model is its internal complexity, as discussed in Rugman and Verbeke (2001, 2003c). The regional aspects identified here further compound this complexity, and this despite the financial markets' demands for transparency and simplicity in strategy and structure. The empirical evidence suggests that MNEs, especially smaller ones, should try to capitalize on opportunities in their home region as far as customer-end activities are concerned, rather than engaging in a path of rapid 'global roll out' of their products and services. A narrow geographic market focus may thus be required as much as a narrow product focus, so as to guarantee the presence of FSAs capable of providing maximum value added to customers, without the need for additional, one-sided, location-specific investments.

Second, from a strategic management perspective, a key problem associated with attempts to implement the transnational solution is the implicit assumption that every activity in the firm requires a careful analysis of its need for location-bound versus non-location-bound company strengths, and resulting managerial decisions to develop and deploy such strengths. The managerial reality, however, is that not all individual activities conducted in the MNE require FSAs instrumental to outperforming rivals, or requiring location-specific adaptation investments abroad. It is therefore important to identify those activities for which FSAs are critical to success, and that may require location-specific adaptation investments abroad. In addition, various combinations of location-bound and non-location-bound strengths may lead to equivalent performance outcomes. Hence, it is necessary to first identify those activities for which access to specific FSA bundles, and location-specific adaptation investments, are critical to the MNE's ultimate economic performance (in terms of market penetration and profitability). In addition, as noted above, it is likely that many of the identified upstream and customer-end activities will require a different composition of FSA bundles, and location-specific adaptation investments, but even if this requisite variety imposed by the external environment can be correctly assessed, this does not guarantee market success. Market success requires three more conditions to be fulfilled: first, the appropriate bundling of critical activities with similar FSA requirements in properly functioning organizational units; second, the effective coordination among these units; third, the differentiation of these units across geographic regions, as a reflection of the MNE's idiosyncratic market position in each region, and the differential need for location-specific adaptation investments in each region.

Third, even in allegedly global functions, such as finance (due to the result of liberalized financial capital markets) there are elements of regionalization that need to be examined. Here are three:

1. The world financial system is now largely dominated in terms of financial intermediation by the three major currencies: the US dollar, the euro and the yen. The pound sterling is increasingly affiliated

with the euro, reflecting British exports of 64 per cent with the rest of the EU and 50 per cent of its inward FDI stock in 1999 from there (Rugman and Kudina, 2002).

2. The leading stock markets appear to largely serve local companies. For example 91 per cent of the new issues on the US NASDAQ are by US companies; in the German Neuer Market 83 per cent of new issues were German, and most of the remaining ones were by other EU companies.

3. The foreign exchange traders in New York and Tokyo exhibited strong isomorphic behaviour guided by home-country patterns of legitimate behaviour, according to Zaheer (1995). Even in a perfect market with instantaneous transmission of information, American foreign exchange traders behaved differently from Japanese traders. Hence, even for tasks and functional areas for which the non-location-bound nature of successful patterns of decisions and actions is widely accepted in the firm, it may be necessary to revisit the old assumption of international transferability. Specifically, the location-specific adaptation investments needed to meld FSAs and CSAs in particular foreign markets may be influenced to an important extent by the MNE's country of origin (Zaheer and Mosakowski, 1997). In other words, a home-region competence may lead to a host-region competence trap.

Fourth, the largest service companies appear even less global than manufacturing companies. In retail, only one of the largest 49 retail firms is global (LVMH), and only five are bi-regional (Rugman and Girod, 2003). In banking, all the 500 companies have the vast majority of their assets in the home region; for example, Citigroup has 80 per cent of its assets in North America. Insurance is even more local. Even knowledge-intensive service industries are largely local. For example, professional service firms, such as law firms, consultants, accountants, etc. are usually embedded in local clusters, with partners being largely immobile and their loose networks being, at best, regionally based.

This situation was anticipated by Campbell and Verbeke (1994), who assessed the validity of the transnational solution for service MNEs. They concluded that the potential for scope economies resulting from the transfer of non-location-bound FSAs is usually lower in service firms, because of the impossibility in many cases of separating the upstream and customer-end segments of the value chain (inseparability of production and delivery). In this context, this implies that regional-market responsiveness at the customer end is only possible if innovation at the upstream end is also decentralized. In other words, decentralization of decision-making power to the regional level may require that large sets of decisions be delegated to that level, and this is usually associated with high, location-specific adaptation investments. Such investments thus imply, paradoxically, a reduction rather than an increase of the MNE's globalization approach at the upstream end, namely if upstream practices appropriate in a host region differ from the home region (e.g. in case of the required use of local resources and network participants).

Fifth, if MNEs face a higher liability of foreignness in customer-end activities as compared to upstream activities, this has two managerial implications from a dynamic perspective. First, learning in the sense of lowering the liability of foreignness, through location-specific adaptation investments in market knowledge, occurs at a different pace in particular activities of the value chain. Foreign market penetration success ultimately is constrained by the activity area with the lowest rate of learning (or the highest required level of location-specific adaptation investments). Managers should thus try to identify the most constraining activities in the critical time paths to achieve international market growth. Second, whereas upstream activities can often be appropriately upgraded, in the sense of successfully linking the MNE's initial set of FSAs with foreign CSAs, as a result of (inexpensive) observational learning and selective imitation, this does not appear so simple at the customer end. Hence, Ohmae (1985) may be correct when he suggests that the deep market penetration of host-triad regions should be performed by collaborative instruments (consortia, joint ventures, etc.). These lead to rapid local embeddedness and access to social network ties. However, collaborating with foreign partners and permitting foreign affiliates to develop local network ties, though avoiding the need for high, location-specific adaptation investments, brings its own set of managerial problems. First is the danger of FSA dissipation through intentional appropriation by the foreign partner, but also in a broader sense through knowledge diffusion as a result of proximity-induced imitation (Hamel et al., 1989). Second is the danger of reduced coherence within the MNE, if affiliates become locally embedded in host-region networks at the expense of the MNE's overall institutionalization logic (Campbell and Verbeke, 2001). The challenges above reflect critical trade-offs to be made, much in line with the decision-making challenges on product diversification in large firms (Ollinger, 1994).

Implications of regionalization for society

The implications of MNE activity for societal welfare and public policy have been the subject of a particularly large and varied literature in economics and political science (Rugman and Verbeke, 1998). The topic of the integration impacts resulting from regional trade and investment agreements has been studied extensively, especially in the context of North American and European integration processes; see Pomfret (2001) for an extensive review. Much of the relevant literature has focused on two issues. First, the problem of trade creation versus trade diversion, whereby insiders and outsiders may be affected differently by a regional integration programme, building upon the seminal work of Viner (1950). Second, the relative merits of regionalization vis-à-vis efforts towards multilateralism, such as through the General Agreement on Tariffs and Trade (GATT) and the World Trade Organization (WTO).

Here, four contradictory perspectives have been formulated (Poon, 1997). First, an emphasis on the economic inferiority of regional vis-à-vis multilateral integration outcomes (Bhagwati, 2002). Second, the view that regionalism is an efficient substitute for ill-functioning multilateral institutions in terms of economic outcomes (Rugman and Verbeke, 2003a). Third, a focus on the comparative ease of conducting a regional integration process (with only a limited number of participants that are geographically close) vis-à-vis a multilateral integration process that could involve all the 144 countries in the WTO. Fourth, a focus on the organic nature of economic integration in regional clusters (Krugman, 1993; Frankel et al., 1995). Here, regional integration is not driven primarily by the strategic intent of government agencies and powerful economic actors to increase or consolidate economic exchange within a region through new institutions in a top-down fashion. Rather, it reflects bottom-up efforts by a multitude of economic actors, who wish to expand their geographical business horizon, guided by immediate opportunities that are geographically close and associated with low transaction costs, as well as a high potential for agglomeration economies. In the long run, such agglomeration, in the sense of improved 'regional diamond conditions' may improve the MNEs' capabilities to penetrate other triad markets (Rugman and Verbeke, 2003b).

None of these four perspectives has paid much attention to the MNE as the appropriate unit of analysis, with some exceptions that include Rugman and Verbeke (1990a, b, 1991), Rugman et al. (1990) and Rugman (1994). This is a fruitful avenue for future IB research, for five reasons.

First, the role of individual MNEs in the institutional processes of regional integration could be investigated in more depth, without starting from the ideological assumption that all MNEs pursue a narrow and homogeneous business agenda. Each firm's regional integration preferences and role will depend upon its FSA configuration, much in line with its preferences regarding trade and investment protection at the national level (Milner, 1988; Salorio, 1993). These preferences may even vary from business to business in a single firm (Rugman et al., 1990). As implied by earlier sections of this chapter, the main question for the MNE is to assess how regional integration may reduce the need for location-specific adaptation investments in the various national markets, when expanding the geographic scope of activities.

Second, rather than merely analysing macroeconomic or sectoral data, there is a rich avenue of work to be pursued on firm-level adaptation processes to regional integration, with a focus on the region-specific adaptation investments that are needed to link the MNE's existing FSAs (non-location-bound and location-bound ones) with the regional-location advantages, and on the nature of these investments (internal development versus external acquisition) (Rugman and Verbeke, 1991). An analysis of such new knowledge development in MNEs may be critical to understand fully the societal effects of increased regionalization.

Third, the impacts of regional trading agreements have often been interpreted in terms of changes in entry barriers facing insiders and outsiders, at the macro, industry and strategic-group levels. From a resource-based perspective, however, there is a real need to understand how regional integration processes affect the creation or elimination of isolating mechanisms, and thereby economic performance, at the level of individual MNEs and subunits within MNEs.

Fourth, regional integration also has implications for knowledge exchange, as it is likely to increase the geographic reach of MNE networks in terms of backward and forward linkages, and even the

MNEs broader flagship networks (Rugman and D'Cruz, 2000). To the extent that such linkages and networks are associated with knowledge diffusion spillovers, these should also be taken into account in any analysis of the regional integration welfare effects.

Finally, regional integration can have an impact on the MNE's internal distribution of resources and FSAs; more specifically, firm-level investments in regional adaptation often imply the relocation of specific production facilities to the most efficient subunits, in order to capture regional scale economies and a reassessment of subsidiary charters. This implies to some extent a zero sum game with 'winning' and 'losing' subsidiaries.

Interestingly, it has also been observed that regional integration may energize subsidiaries to start new initiatives and to develop new capabilities, which really implies a non-zero sum game (Birkinshaw, 2000), again with macro-level welfare improvements as an outcome. Will the deepening of a regional trading block, even if it has positive net welfare effects inside the region and at the world level, strengthen the affected insider MNEs in other legs of the triad? Or will it, on the contrary, act as an incentive to focus these MNEs' resource allocation processes and market expansion plans even more on intra-regional growth opportunities? The empirical data presented in this chapter appear to indicate that regional integration during the past decade has had little effect on the abilities of MNEs to increase their globalization capabilities.

Conclusions

The evidence is that most of the world's largest firms are stay-at-home multinationals. The great majority of MNEs (320 out of 380 with available data) have, on average, 80 per cent of all their sales in their home region of the triad. The world of international business is a regional one, not a global one. Only a handful of MNEs (a total of nine) actually operate successfully as key players in each region of the triad. For 320 of 365 cases of MNEs for which data are available, the data indicate they operate on a home-triad basis. This is very strong evidence of regional/triad activity. There are 25 bi-regional MNEs and another 11 host-country based ones. There are so few 'global' MNEs as to render the concept of 'globalization' meaningless. This research suggests that scholars of international business need to pay less attention to models of 'global' strategy – as this is a special case. The 'big question' for research in international business is: why do MNEs succeed as regional organizations without becoming global?

Transaction cost economics reasoning largely explains this phenomenon: market-seeking expansion in host regions is often associated with high, location-specific adaptation investments to link the MNE's existing knowledge base with host-region location advantages. FSAs and CSAs do not simply meld together without managerial intervention. As the required investments to meld FSAs and CSAs become larger, driven by the cultural, administrative, geographic and economic distance between home country/region and host regions, the attractiveness of foreign markets declines, and regional, rather than global, strategies are needed to reflect the differential need for 'linking' investments in each region. Only in a few sectors, such as consumer electronics, can a balanced, global distribution of sales be achieved.

It is likely that the upstream end of the value chain can be globalized more easily than the customer end, which has been the focus of this chapter, because upstream location-specific investments are not one-sided (in the sense of lacking reciprocal commitments from the other economic actors involved, which is a critical problem at the customer end). Upstream globalization obviously need not be expressed in a balanced geographic distribution of R&D, manufacturing, etc., but rather in the MNE's ability to choose and access locations around the globe where the firm's upstream FSAs can easily be melded with foreign location advantages, without the need for major, location-specific adaptation investments. Yet, the available data on production also suggest the importance of home-region based production clusters and networks, as in the automobile sector, thus indicating that the hazards of cultural, administrative, geographic and economic distance between the home country/region and host regions are often also present at the upstream side.

References

Bartlett, C. and Ghoshal, S. (1989) *Managing across Borders: the Transnational Solution*. Boston, Mass.: Harvard Business School Press.

Bhagwati, J. (2002) *Free Trade Today*. Princeton, NJ: Princeton University Press.

Birkinshaw, J. (2000) *Entrepreneurship in the Global Firm*. London: Sage.

Buckley, P. (2002) 'Is the International Business Research Agenda Running Out of Steam?' , *Journal of International Business Studies*, 33(2): 365–73.

Campbell, A. and Verbeke A. (1994) 'The Globalization of Service Multinationals', *Long Range Planning*, 27(2): 95–102.

Campbell, A. and Verbeke, A. (2001) 'The Multinational Management of Multiple External Network', in D. Van den Bulcke and A. Verbeke (eds), *Globalisation and the Small Open Economy*, Cheltenham: E. Elgar, 193–209.

Dunning, J. H. (1993) *The Globalization of Business*. London: Routledge.

Frankel, J., Stein, E. and Wei, S. J. (1995) 'Trading Blocs and the Americas: the Natural, the Unnatural and the Super-natural', *Journal of Development Economics*, 47: 61–95.

Ghemawat, P. (2001) 'Distance Still Matters: the Hard Reality of Global Expansion', *Harvard Business Review*, 79(8) (September): 137–47.

Ghemawat, P. (2003) 'Semiglobalization and International Business Strategy', *Journal of International Business Studies*, doi:10.1057/palgrave.jibs.8400013.

Hamel, G., Doz,Y. and Prahalad, C. K. (1989) 'Collaborate with Your Competitors and Win', *Harvard Business Review*, 67(1): 133–9.

Johansson, J. and Vahlne, J. E. (1977) 'The Internationalization Process of the Firm: a Model of Knowledge Development and Increasing Foreign Market Commitments', *Journal of International Business Studies*, 8(1): 23–32.

Johansson, J. and Vahlne, J. E. (1990) 'The Mechanism of Internationalization', *International Marketing Review*, 7(4): 1–24.

Krugman, P. (1993) 'Regionalism versus Multilateralism: Analytical Note' in J. de Melo and A. Panagarily (eds), *New Dimensions in Regional Integration*, New York: Cambridge University Press, 58–79.

Levitt, T. (1983) 'The Globalization of Markets', *Harvard Business Review*, May–June: 92–102.

Milner, H. V. (1988) *Resisting Protectionism: Global Industries and the Policies of International Trade*, Princeton, NJ: Princeton University Press.

Ohmae, K. (1985) *Triad Power: the Coming Shape of Global Competition*. New York: The Free Press.

Ollinger, M. (1994) 'The Limits of Growth of the Multidivisional Firm: a Case Study of the U.S. Oil Industry from 1930–90', *Strategic Management Journal*, 15(7): 503–20.

Pomfret, R. (2001) *The Economics of Regional Trading Arrangements*. University of Oxford: Oxford University Press.

Poon, J. (1997) 'The Cosmopolitanization of Trade Regions: Global Trends and Implications', *Economic Geography*, 73: 390–404.

Porter M. (1990) *The Competitive Advantage of Nations*, Free Press: New York.

Rugman A. M. (1981) *Inside the Multinationals*. New York: Columbia University Press.

Rugman, A. M. (ed.) (1994) *Foreign Investment and NAFTA*. Columbia, SC: University of South Carolina Press.

Rugman, A. M. (1996) *The Theory of Multinational Enterprises*. Cheltenham: Elgar.

Rugman, A. M. (2000) *The End of Globalization*. London: Random House and New York: Amacom-McGraw Hill.

Rugman, A.M. and D'Cruz, J. (2000) *Multinationals as Flagship Firms: Regional Business Networks*. Oxford: Oxford University Press.

Rugman, A. M. and Girod, S. (2003) 'Retail Multinationals and Globalization: the Evidence is Regional', *European Management Review*, 21(1): 24–37.

Rugman, A. M. and Kudina, A. (2002) 'Britain, Europe and North America' in M. Fratianni et al. (eds), *Governing Global Finance*, Aldershot, UK: Ashgate, 185–95.

Rugman, A. M. and Verbeke, A. (1990a) *Global Corporate Strategy and Trade Policy*. London and New York: Routledge.

Rugman, A. M. and Verbeke, A. (1990b) 'Strategic Planning, Adjustment and Trade Liberalisation' in A. Rugman (ed.), *Multinationals and Canada–United States Free Trade*, Columbia, SC: University of South Carolina Press, 146–78.

Rugman, A. M. and Verbeke, A. (1991) 'Environmental Change and Global Competitive Strategy in Europe' in A. Rugman and A. Verbeke (eds), *Global Competition and the European Community*, Greenwich, Conn.: JAI Press, 3–28.

Rugman, A. M. and. Verbeke, A. (1992) 'A Note on the Transnational Solution and the Transaction Cost Theory of Multinational Strategic Management', *Journal of International Business Studies*, 23(4): 761–71.

Rugman, A. M. and Verbeke, A. (eds) (1995) *Global Competition: Beyond the Diamond. Research in Global Strategic Management*. Greenwich, Conn.: JAI Press Inc.

Rugman, A. M. and Verbeke, A. (1998) 'Multinational Enterprises and Public Policy', *Journal of International Business Studies*, 29(1): 115–36.

Rugman, A. M. and Verbeke, A. (2001) 'Subsidiary-specific Advantages in Multinational Enterprises', *Strategic Management Journal*, 22(3): 237–50.

Rugman, A. M. and Verbeke, A. (2003a) 'The World Trade Organization, Multinational Enterprises, and the Civil Society', in M. Fratianni, P. Savona and J. Kirton (eds) *Sustaining Global Growth and Development*, Aldershot, UK: Ashgate, 81–97.

Rugman, A. and Verbeke, A. (2003b) 'Multinational Enterprises and Clusters: an Organizing Framework', *Management International Review*, Special Issue 3: 151–69.

Rugman, A. and Verbeke, A. (2003c) 'Extending the Theory of the Multinational Enterprise: Internalization and Strategic Management Perspectives', *Journal of International Business Studies*, 34(2): 125–37.

Rugman, A. M. and Verbeke, A. (2004) 'A Perspective on Regional and Global Strategies of Multinational Enterprises', *Journal of International Business Studies*, 35(1): 1–15.

Rugman, A. M., Verbeke, A. and Luxmore, S. (1990) 'Corporate Strategy and the Free Trade Agreement: Adjustment by Canadian Multinational Enterprises', *Canadian Journal of Regional Science*, 13 (2/3): 307–30.

Salorio E. (1993) 'Strategic Use of Import Protection: Seeking Shelter for Competitive Advantage', in A. M. Rugman and A. Verbeke (eds), *Beyond the Three Generics*, Greenwich, Conn.: JAI Press, 101–24.

Viner, J. (1950) *The Customs Union Issue*. New York: Carnegie Endowment for International Peace.

Zaheer, S. (1995) 'Overcoming the Liability of Foreignness', *Academy of Management Journal*, 38(2): 341–63.

Zaheer, S. and Mosakowski, E. (1997) 'The Dynamics of the Liability of Foreignness: a Global Study of Survival in Financial Services', *Strategic Management Journal*, 18(6): 439–64.

8

What is International Business? An Economic Historian's View

Mira Wilkins

International business is an institutional structure. The noun is business (often used in this chapter, and in the general literature, interchangeably with firm, company, corporation, enterprise). The purpose of business is to produce goods and services. The business is the actor. It is not a 'black box', but a package of managed attributes. The adjective is international (often used in this chapter, and in the literature, interchangeably with multinational, transnational, global). The modifier covers the crossing of country borders. Combining the adjective with the noun, an international business is an entity that produces goods and/or services over such boundaries.

The word 'business' embraces the gamut of enterprises, including banks and other financial intermediaries. International, multinational, transnational and global (as I use the adjectives) are not ranked. Other authors have done so, but, by now within the literature, the confusion is so great, it is best to apply the designations interchangeably.

An international business makes foreign direct investments; typically (albeit far from always), the latter are in an affiliate that will be incorporated (registered) in the recipient, 'host' country with a hierarchical pattern between the parent and affiliate. An international business is a tissue of associated units (branches, corporations) that join the headquarters in the 'home' country (or less often two or, rarely, three home countries) with units in one or, now very frequently, numerous host countries. I define home as the country locale of the parent firm and host that of the country abroad. International businesses change over time in a broad overall social, economic and political context. They are impacted by and, in turn, in varying dimensions, have influence on the evolving external environment. Nothing is static. Change occurs within and outside the business (and the two interact). Change is, moreover, not uniform within (or outside) the business. For example, if political frontiers are redrawn, an individual company can become international without 'doing' anything, or alternatively can become national as a once foreign territory is brought within a home country's borders. For the historian, this represents part of the general recognition that no company operates immune from outside change. While I defined international business as that of the firm over political borders, other authors have considered international business as 'an activity'.[1] This is fine, but it is not my definition nor what I seek to understand. I am viewing individual firms across politically established country frontiers.

What then is international business? It is a business – with all the attributes that a business entails – that traverses country borders and evolves over time, sometimes dropping by the wayside, sometimes expanding greatly (through internal expansion or through mergers, or both), sometimes contracting in part, spinning off or being ordered to divest certain parts. Voluntary divestments can be for perceived efficiency purposes; they can be to satisfy immediate needs for revenues; involuntary ones can be for many reasons ranging from nationalization to antitrust. Sometimes, an enterprise simultaneously expands in one direction and restructures, shutting down other operations.

Over time, the largest international businesses become multi-functional, multi-product, multi-process, geographically extended enterprises operating often in a number of different 'sectors' (industrial categories) and in a multitude of countries. The single international business involves a cluster of units (some but not all of which will be separate corporations). Growth and its direction are always uneven. Moreover, expansion has no inevitability. Many international businesses were larger (in terms of assets, sales, employment and/or market capitalization) at some past time than today. Many international businesses of times past no longer exist in the present. Also, often the edges of the firm are porous and can be ill-defined. It is not infrequent (or inappropriate) to discuss firms within an international business, ones that have developed their own history and traditions. An individual international business may have a joint venture with another firm in one market or one activity, yet be very competitive with that 'partner' on a global basis. Today's international business are complex entities.

Understanding the history of an international business provides a lens on world history and also a means of understanding the strategies and structures of today's global business. It is common for historians to discuss comparative histories, comparing national experiences. International business, by contrast, must be understood in the context of the relationships between and among nations through time. Added to comparisons are the interactions, the interface. Intra-firm transactions are multiple and within an international business there is both outward diffusion from the parent of products and processes, of explicit and tacit knowledge – and also 'reverse diffusion', where affiliates contribute to the enrichment of the parent and to the entire global enterprise.[2]

To understand what is international business, a recognition of change must be a paramount consideration. Through time, business strategies are affected by five fundamentals:

1. *Economic opportunities.* Investments are made when businessmen perceive some type of economic opportunity.

2. *Political considerations.* On the one hand, political conditions can obstruct investments, economic opportunities notwithstanding; on the other hand, a promising political environment can encourage investment.

3. *Familiarity. Ceteris paribus*, the more familiar a locale, the more readily (in a sequence) investments will be made. Familiarity can be geographic, linguistic, cultural and/or grounded in historical experience. It serves to reduce risk.

4. *Third country aspects.* Investments can be motivated by business plans that do not relate specifically to the home or to the host country, but rather to a third country or countries. An example would be an investment within the European Union spurred by the region's market potential – outside the national locale of the investor (the home country) and the investment (the host country).

5. *Internal enterprise background, core competencies and leadership.* Each international business makes decisions at any point in time based on the configurations of earlier ones. Business history matters.[3]

International business history

International business arose initially when seller and buyer were separated by political frontiers. The earliest international business was an outcome of the trade of ancient times, when a merchant required a representative abroad (in a host locale) to handle (to receive, warehouse and distribute) goods. If this individual was part of the merchant's family or had an ongoing regular connection with the merchant who continued to be headquartered in the home country, an international business structure could be identified.[4] There was an economic imperative in extending the firm over borders. Our definition of the business as a producer of goods and services encompasses the trading firm, which produces services. Merchants provided the basis for the first international businesses. International businesses have 'to begin', so a firm's presence that stretches over boundaries, however small that presence may be, I would consider to be that of an international business. Historians have argued that you cannot have 'international' business in an era before nation states. I have fine-tuned my definition so as to define international as the crossing over political borders of countries and, I could add (to be inclusive, city states), so this contention would not a priori rule out the early international businesses. In more modern times, there is the problem of business in colonies. Once more, I stretch the definition of 'countries' to include those countries within the large overseas empires of Britain, France and Holland, for example.

It is possible to document a variety of international businesses before we focus in on the modern ones that emerged in the late nineteenth century. How does the modern multinational enterprise differ from those of past centuries? What are the characteristics of modern international business? An international business involves coordination and possibilities of control of extended business units and their functions. It consists of transfers within the firm of part or all of the 'package' of attributes that constitute the business enterprise. Without the key innovations of the nineteenth century in transportation and communications, coordination and control had to be based solely on trust, accepted values and organizational culture. Many of the early trading units, and subsequent banking partnerships, seem to have lacked hierarchy; there was delegation and coincidence in functions. This institutional form persisted into the nineteenth and the twentieth centuries, overlapping with the modern international business. Thus, the Rothschild houses in England and the continent, certainly operated as part of an international business, even though home and host were ill-defined.

Sometimes, with the pre-modern international businesses, the East India Company, for instance, home and hosts were clear; hierarchy was evident; yet when the large chartered trading corporations sent individuals abroad, communications took months. There had to be conditioning, understanding, because close supervision was impossible. The notions of trust, accepted values and organizational culture persist within modern multinational enterprises, but for the modern international business they are insufficient. Transactions are governed more directly. And, the number of transactions dwarfs that of the early international enterprises.

When steamships traversed the Atlantic in the mid-nineteenth century and railroads began to penetrate the interiors of nations, after cables girded the world and became connected with national telegraph systems, distances were increasingly compressed. The world became smaller. 'Speed' in transportation and communications for the first time supplied the infrastructure (the underpinnings) required to manage the modern multinational enterprise. Further innovations in transportation and communications to follow would make for an even smaller world. But it was these late nineteenth-century beginnings that made possible new coordination and control. What could be and what was moved within the modern enterprise (products, processes, ideas, knowledge, people, capital and so forth) expanded exponentially. For the modern international business, scholars can draw different diagrams for a single business's corporate ownership, administration, operations (including financing, process and product design, trade flows for end products and inputs, personnel policies and so forth). These diagrams alter through time in a non-linear manner.

The earliest international businesses were traders, and then banks, insurance companies, and individuals who joined to form groups that had extended over borders to do business outside the home country; in some cases manufacturing abroad was included. Yet, it was not until the nineteenth century, with modern international business, that manufacturing companies extended themselves over borders to become international businesses.[5] The rise of modern international business coincided with the development of sizeable domestic industrial enterprises, businesses that expanded beyond a single site locale and increasingly internalized within the firm ways of connecting the producer with the consumers. Among the pioneering modern multinational enterprises that had their origins before the First World

War, in the late nineteenth or early twentieth centuries, were companies such as Singer Sewing Machine, the Standard Oil group, Royal Dutch Shell, International Harvester, American Tobacco (and then British American Tobacco Company), Lever Brothers, Nestlé, United Fruit, General Electric, Siemens, Allgemeine Elektrizitäts Gesellschaft (AEG), Hoffmann-La Roche, Bayer and Ford Motor Company. These businesses were headquartered in the United States or western Europe. They were innovative enterprises that introduced new products and processes – and new techniques to market their output. They were in a range of industries, but each company developed a competitive advantage that I would argue stemmed not from 'monopoly' power, but from efficiencies. All these companies combined production of goods with the distribution of the output; all in a modern sense developed management of the extended business.[6] In addition, in the late nineteenth and early twentieth centuries, trading companies and banking institutions, headquartered principally in western Europe and Japan, became modern international businesses.[7] British banks, such as the Hongkong and Shanghai Banking Corporation, were key international businesses. In Japan before the First World War, there were some modern international businesses in manufacturing (in textiles), but globally these were insignificant and were dwarfed by such large international businesses as the Yokohama Specie Bank and Mitsui & Co. All these were business enterprises. They expected revenues to exceed costs, i.e. they expected to make profits. Did they 'profit maximize'? Probably not.[8]

Why did such firms become international businesses? Which ones were able to sustain international business into the twenty-first century? The answers help us with our basic question on What is international business? Practically all the manufacturing companies enumerated above undertook domestic business at the same time as they became international.[9] There is an important difference between trade and investment. In some cases the international investments complemented exports; in some cases the investments substituted for exports; and in other cases they had nothing to do with exports. In some cases, they were associated with imports; more often, they were not. There were major asymmetries.

The five fundamentals outlined earlier in this essay were very much in evidence. All of these companies extended internationally to take advantage of economic opportunities and to pursue these opportunities.

Political obstacles to their extension existed, with the most dramatic the US antitrust cases of 1911 (a home country rather than host country obstacle). Yet, the very same antitrust cases, which had a profound impact on the Standard Oil companies, in international business opened the way for Royal Dutch Shell's US business. Tariffs, for example, which pushed certain of the industrial enterprises to prefer foreign manufacturing to exports represented a political element, influencing plant location choices. Political considerations in some instances discouraged foreign direct investments, and in others encouraged it. Familiarity was very much in evidence with US companies making direct investments in the geographically near Caribbean region and in the culturally and historically familiar Canada (which was also geographically nearby) as well Great Britain. The map of German companies' foreign direct investments, for example, was very different from that of US business abroad. Third-country considerations influenced the arrangements that Ford Motor Company made with its Canadian plant in 1904 (one year after the founding the company); the Canadian Ford company was allocated as territory of the British empire, so the facility could achieve economies of scale.[10] As corporate legacies were established, the pattern of expansion was influenced. Already, before 1914, within Germany Siemens and AEG had very different strategies in their business abroad, based on their prior experiences. As we ask what is an international business, it seems to be a business that, at some point in its history, perceived that it had a competitive advantage in investing abroad. It then proceeded – at different paces and with no guarantees of success. Country locations and industries shaped practices, but individual firm responses also diverged.[11]

Intra-company coordination and control

In defining what is international business, economists and statisticians have looked to questions of ownership and control. As indicated above, international businesses make foreign direct investments, which a recent *World Investment Report* defined

> as an investment involving a long-term relationship and reflecting a lasting interest and control by a resident entity in one economy (foreign direct investor or parent enterprise) in an economy other

than that of the foreign direct investor (FDI enterprise or affiliate enterprise or foreign affiliate)....An equity capital stake of 10 per cent or more of the ordinary shares or voting power for an incorporated enterprise, or its equivalent for an unincorporated enterprise, is normally considered as a threshold for the control of assets.[12]

Such thresholds are required for gathering uniform statistics, but they fail to address the nuances of ownership and control, which are essential to consider in comprehending what is international business. Control is a very illusory concept. In broad terms, economists' discussions of principal/agency relationships are highly germane.[13] Since a modern international business involves a cluster of companies, with a parent having ownership (foreign direct investments) and representing the 'principal', the management of each affiliated unit becomes in principal/agency terms the 'agent(s)'. And, just as is the case in the purely domestic situation, it is even more likely when business over borders is involved that the agent abroad may well have a separate agenda. The parent's ability to exercise control is always constrained.

In understanding the nature of international business, it must be recognized that affiliates abroad develop through time their own distinct histories and the degree and nature of 'control' exercised by the parent vary substantially over functions and most important over time. It may be related to the extent of ownership. Size of ownership may not matter, however, on a day-to-day basis. Ownership only provides 'potential' for control (ultimately to dismiss the top management of the subsidiary and appoint new management), but even these choices may be highly limited, for the opportunity cost of exercising such an option may exceed the perceived benefit.

This has many implications in the clarification of what is international business. Because a single international business is a complex institutional form, it may speak on some matters with more than one voice. Intra-company transactions need to be studied, always keeping in mind that the fundamental motivations are those of the business enterprise, but that within the large enterprise, intra-company bargaining for resources must be studied within a framework of the history of the international business as well as the changing economic and political environment. Consumer choices can be influenced by the large enterprise, but businesses no matter how big often find themselves at the mercy of unpredictable events. This is true domestically, yet far more important internationally. Principals and agents may (and often do) have separate responses to change.

International business and capital flows

Frequently, international business is associated with international flows of capital. Yet, there is far from synchronization. Because the international business is a package of business attributes, capital is only one of them. A large multinational enterprise has flexibility to mobilize capital from where it is most accessible (and at least cost). It may borrow locally or in third countries (that is not in the parent country). It may grow in some nations based on reinvested earnings. In other countries, where currencies are losing value, it may remit profits as quickly as possible and only add new capital resources when there is immediate need.

Like any business, international businesses assemble capital for productive purposes. Where that capital comes from can and does vary substantially – across space as well as time. What is fundamental is that the business is *motivated* to employ the capital in an efficient manner. It may not do so for a range of reasons, from those of government interventions to those of principal/agent problems. Basically, however, if we define an international business as a business that crosses borders, we see it as trying to do internationally what it does best, i.e. gather the inputs, including capital, to produce the goods and services about which it has knowledge and experience.

International business and knowledge flows: hybrid management

International business can be thought of a package, combining resources to produce goods and/or services. With international business, by definition, knowledge is defused within an organization. And because the parent has (or perceives it has) a competitive advantage, typically the knowledge flows have stemmed from parent outward. However, as international business has evolved there came to be a two-way street, where the parent obtained knowledge from an existing affiliate or a newly acquired one. This only works if the parent has sufficient competence to absorb the knowledge. Buying technology does not suffice, if the parent is unable to use it effectively. To repeat, the history of international business records successes and failures, continuities and discontinuities.[14]

Within an international business, there is always the important issue of application and adaptation. As an international business expands, it meets new conditions in different nations abroad. Application of home methods of doing business, replicating what has been done before, gives the foreign firm a cost advantage. Yet, adaptation is often required, owing to very different conditions in the host country. But a firm that adapts to conditions abroad may be raising its costs, and worse still dissipating its initial advantage. The give and take between application and adaptation is highly nuanced. Some years ago, Professor Tetsuo Abo came up with the notion of 'hybrid factories'. He argued that in the 1970s and 1980s the Japanese advantage in international business was in the factory processes; if these were changed substantially, there would be a loss of advantage. He looked at Japanese business abroad, and the extent of application and adaptation.[15] Abo saw adaptation as introducing new costs, but at times clearly necessary. His research stimulated others and the term 'hybridization' was expanded beyond the factory to general management issues. While there continued to be recognition that the costs of adaptation might be high, there was a weighing of the costs of lack of adaptation.[16] Studies showed adaptation to be very different in different companies and different settings, even within a single industry. There came to be a recognition that 'It is not possible simply to define a single most efficient model and then diffuse it.'[17] Learning comes from a variety of sources. Pragmatic adaptations of a transferred method might indeed over time lead to significant innovation and instead of having negative consequences, adaptations could achieve far superior results. In addition, within an international business, 'reverse learning may be as important as diffusion'.[18]

Seen in this light, too much adaptation abroad could be negative (i.e. reducing the business advantage), but extensive adaptation abroad also could be positive both in the host country environment and also in its feedbacks to the parent (i.e. improving the advantage). While the notion of hybridization in its original usage dealt with the factory management, the new thinking is about hybridization of overall firm management and emphasizes a very important feature of international business. Where ever and when ever an international business goes abroad, it applies and adapts; it learns. International trade theory tells us that there are gains from trade. So, too, the new thinking about hybridization suggests gains from international business in the international transfers of knowledge tested in differing environments. The gains do not come from specialization (as in international trade theory) but rather from the sharing and merging of knowledge within a business framework; imitation and innovation combine with an improved product, process, or purchasing, or marketing, or advertising or financing strategy. Hybrid management seen in this way internalizes within individual firms, what has been increasingly suggested by economic development experts, that the best growth patterns arise from copying and surpassing, imitating and innovating, emulating and diversifying. The individual international business is in an enviable position to do that. The applications and adaptations, the hybridization, have to be seen both through time and space. Hybridization needs to be analysed in the context of the difficulties in defining 'control'. It is intimately associated with bargaining within the international business – and also with the principal/agency dilemma. New research suggests that at times the agent may know best, albeit the principal's involvement is very much a requirement. Management matters.

When HSBC (the old Hongkong and Shanghai Banking Corporation) advertises that it has offices in 79 countries and territories, Europe, Asia Pacific, the Americas, the Middle East and Africa, each staffed by local people, it is doing what international businesses have done over years.

> Being local enables them [the local offices] to offer insights into financial opportunities and create service initiatives that would never occur to an outsider. It means our customers get the kind of local knowledge and personal service that you'd expect of a local bank. And a level of global knowledge and widely sourced expertise that you wouldn't.[19]

The last sentence is key to the 'application'. The HSBC advertises the positive nature of 'hybridization', the combining of core competencies (which now are 'widely sourced') with 'local knowledge': Diffusion, reverse diffusion, but more, international diffusion within the firm.

The passage of time

What happened to the pioneer modern multinational enterprises that began before the First World War, which we mentioned earlier in this chapter? Did many survive to the start of the twenty-first century? Which ones did and what sorts of new entries have there been? Some of these pioneer modern international businesses were in industries that lost their relative importance. In the twenty-first century, ready-made clothing is everywhere available. Indeed the new international businesses are the GAP and Banana Republic. Singer Sewing Machine went bankrupt, was (in 1989) taken over by a Hong Kong entrepreneur, whose company in turn went bankrupt. Singer is no longer an important actor. It was unable to adapt to changing times.[20]

By contrast, Royal Dutch Shell has kept its prominence through the twentieth century and into the twenty-first century. Standard Oil, after the 1911 break-up, spawned 34 separate companies, nine of which retained foreign business; others became international businesses; they merged with one another (with independents, and foreign international businesses). As a consequence, today's leading companies in the oil industry are an outcome of the late nineteenth century–early twentieth century story, with an uneven course through time. Their corporate histories have been strongly influenced by the past as well as contemporary considerations: BP (an early international business that would in the course of its history absorb several of the original Standard Oil companies), Exxon Mobil (a direct successor to Standard Oil of New Jersey and then a merger with the one-time Standard Oil of New York), and Royal Dutch Shell all rank very high on a roster of today's transnational corporations.[21]

The conditions of world agriculture reduced the relative importance of International Harvester; its name was changed in 1986 to Navistar. Once a giant among the international businesses, it does not now rank in the top 100 transnational corporations listed in the *World Investment Report 2003*.[22] By contrast, British American Tobacco – and its successor BAT Industries (separated from its equity links with American Tobacco in 1911 and from its other 'parent' Imperial Tobacco in 1980) – stayed significant throughout the twentieth and into the twenty-first century.[23]

On the other pioneer firms; some survived and flourished: General Electric and Siemens, for example. These two companies had very different histories. General Electric was remarkable in its adaptation through time and ranked in 2001 as number 2 among the world's top transnational corporations (ranked by foreign assets).[24] Two world wars and other political adversities cut into the continuity of the Siemens enterprise, but the human capital was intact, and there has been a rebirth of the firm. Other businesses fell by the wayside, at different times and in different settings: AEG and United Fruit, for instance. AEG went into bankruptcy, as did United Fruit. The latter revived as Chiquita Banana, a less significant company, especially when compared with its innovative pre-First World War predecessor.[25] Lever Brothers was merged in 1929 into the giant Unilever. Nestlé remained; as it grew, it acquired numerous other companies. Bayer's international business was disrupted during the First World War, resumed, was absorbed into I. G. Farben in the 1920s, lost out during the Second World War, and once more was reborn. Hoffmann-La Roche (now Roche), with ups and downs, continued from its late nineteenth-century origins. And Ford Motor Company was an international business practically from its start to the present. Yet, as in the cases of all the surviving pioneers in international business, its strategies and structures changed greatly over time; different phases in its corporate history in turn influenced the subsequent ones. Indeed, a very interesting example of hybridization lies in the relationship of Ford and Mazda (as of 1996, Ford had sufficient ownership of Mazda to 'exercise control'). Many of the British overseas banks, having gone through dramatic changes over the decades, have survived – as was indicated above with HSBC (the new name is an abbreviation of the traditional bank's name, Hongkong and Shanghai Banking Corporation). Mitsui & Co. is still an important trading firm (following on a significant interruption in its activities in the aftermath of the Second World War). As for Yokohama Specie Bank, it was resurrected after the Second World War as the much smaller Bank of Tokyo, which in 1996 was folded into The Bank of Tokyo-Mitsubishi. Losses in 1998–99 resulted in the formation in 2000 of a financial group with Mitsubishi Trust Bank and Nippon Trust Bank; in 2001 these banks formed Mitsubishi Tokyo Financial Group.[26] If, however, there exist these (and other) Japanese jagged continuities in trading companies and financial institutions, the post-Second World War Japanese newcomers in international business in electronics and automobiles were unprecedented, reflecting new waves of technological change.

What light does this discourse shed on the question, 'What is international business?' It reiterates our argument that international business is an institutional form, with a far from static existence. If one turns over the coin and instead of beginning with the pioneer modern firms, one starts from the list of today's leaders, one comes up with an immense historical variety. Vodafone in telecommunications, a relative newcomer (which dates its 'inception' to 1982), had in 2001 larger foreign assets than any other non-financial transnational corporation. This British enterprise's prominence came with its competitive advantage and its innovative activities in cell phones. It was part of the new information technologies of the late twentieth and early twenty-first centuries. It bears a keen resemblance to other pioneers. Vivendi Universal was a blip in its role on the early twenty-first century lists, but it too is interesting for historically it emerged from two very different roots (a French water supplier and a Canadian beverage company that had diversified into the movie business).

Another newcomer in international business in the early twenty-first century top group is Deutsche Telekom AG, a company with a long and staid domestic history in an industry that with privatization and the new cell phones rapidly came of age as an international business. So, too, on the list of top transnational enterprises, there are the Japanese companies, in particular Toyota Motor Corporation, Honda Motor Corporation and Nissan Motor Corporation (whose 'parent' Renault is separately listed).

Rosters of transnational enterprises often exclude those that offer financial and other services. This is unfortunate. International business is not simply in the manufacturing sector. Understanding international business must include those in the entire range of sectors. From the late nineteenth century to the present, the largest and most successful multinational enterprises have been innovative and adaptive. They have metamorphosed as times have changed. Newcomers have emerged to create new products and processes over a wide spectrum.

Profits and international business

By definition, businesses are expected to make profits in order to survive. Earlier, I argued that international business was motivated to employ capital in an efficient fashion. This assumed that the firm looked to profits, to increasing revenues and decreasing costs (not necessarily in individual countries, but certainly on a global scale). Ultimately, if not in the short run, 'success' in international business meant that individual units contributed to the profitability of the overall enterprise. (The scandals and abuses affecting large multi-national enterprises in the early twenty-first century resulted in losses and failures.)

In the twentieth century, production of goods and services was often by state-owned enterprises, where profits were a low priority – and profitability was not necessarily required for continuity. A number of state-owned enterprises engaged in business abroad.[27] Do they fit into my definition of international business? Clearly, these were producers of goods and services over borders. Clearly, too, at times, the behaviour of these state-owned institutions closely resembled that of private sector activities. Some looked to profitable opportunities (and expected profits). But, even if profits were not the top goal, in the long run these enterprises only did well in their international business, if they were able to develop their competitive advantage. Some were able to do so and sustained their operations abroad. Many failed in this endeavour – or alternatively, only became successful inter-national businesses after they were privatized. I believe it is necessary to include within my definitions, with the appropriate qualifi-cations, government-controlled businesses that extended over political boundaries.

Bias and what is international business

Since our assignment in this volume was to speak to some of the issues addressed by E. H. Carr, in his *What Is History?* and I have done so implicitly in what precedes this section, I have not, however, dealt with the important issue of bias, whether facts speak for themselves or whether as the historian of international business selects facts, a bias is introduced.[28] Clearly, in the massive evidence on international business, the scholar must make selections and choose what he or she believes is important. 'Facts' are collected and assembled from the most reliable sources. The historian of international business knows that memories are fallible; the best sources on the development of international business involve evidence from corporate records of the key decision makers. These may have abbreviated explanations and may need to be carefully supplemented by other sources, for example, personal correspondence of executives and for recent events, reminiscences.

My approach to the study of international business is that this is an important institution. I want to understand it. I try to use contemporary documentation. I understand that individuals at headquarters and those at a subsidiary may perceive the same occurrence in a different light (and indeed, at both headquarters *and* the foreign subsidiary different individuals differ in interpretation). In my view, it is the obligation of the student of international business to write about what happened with as much accuracy as possible. This may mean recording the different perceptions of different participants, and only making judgements when the relevant records become available (here the historian has a major advantage over the contemporary student of international business, for the historian has a perspective on which documents to select and to read). It never means introducing one's own ideological bias onto the material. If, however, the scholar's bias is towards understanding as best one is able, then so be it. Understanding involves deciphering how decision making is done on significant issues. Significance is tricky and here the historian must make judgements.

My interest has tended to concentrate on large international businesses. Small international businesses are numerous and overall they make a difference. Individually, however, particular large international business transformed the twentieth century. I find those 'more important', more interesting, more worthy of study. Yet, that is indeed my bias, and in defining what is international business, there must be the recognition that international businesses can be large and can be small; they can be important (causing economic growth, changing thinking about production processes and products, etc.) and they can be one of a multitude. My bias is to focus on the significant players.

The student of international business does not want to distort. He or she recognizes that not all multinationals are large; not all are successful (either from a firm or from other perspectives). Thus, the students who deal with 'why failure' are handling important questions. For me, however, I am more interested in how the large international business copes with both successes and failures. No large multinational enterprise is always successful (however defined). There are frequent (often partial) failures. A balanced study deals with the why? In defining what is international business, it has to be recognized as an imperfect institution (but all institutions are imperfect), yet established for the purpose of producing goods and services and if a private sector enterprise, making profits in doing so.

Normative and public policy consequences

If we understand what is international business (as described above), the student of international business has still not handled the normative consequences, i.e. made value judgements: is the international business 'good' or 'bad', or good and bad, depending on the circumstances. Have public policies over the years towards international business been appropriate? In defining what is international business, the historian may also want to consider its impact, always recognizing that the actor can be seen as separate from its impact. Part of the impact is often a result, however, of public policies towards the international business. If, as is frequently the case, a government (or the public that the government wishes to represent) does not understand what is international business, if there is a presumption that the international business is 'basically political', or that 'the entity is bound to exploit', or that 'management is irrelevant', or 'that the international business has nothing to offer', or 'that profits are always exorbitant', then such misperceptions of the international business can (and do) result in disadvantageous or dysfunctional public policies. Certainly the historian must explain the genesis of such policies and their consequences. Bad policies and lack of understanding have often been part of the realities that shape decision making. They do not change the answer to what is international business, but do alter the behaviour of the business. Lest I upset my reader, I do not take the position that international businesses never interact with governments; of course, they do in many circumstances; my view is that they are producers of goods and services, economic institutions, and not basically, fundamentally, political ones. I do take the view that by definition they are not bound to exploit, that management is relevant, and that the production of goods and services has a great deal to offer.

Conclusions

International businesses were important actors in twentieth-century history and continue to be important actors in the early twenty-first century. Some such businesses are far more important than others, having because of their new technologies, new methods and their management, introduced on a global scale unprecedented change. They have served as allocators of global resources. They have created new investments and with them new employment opportunities. They have provided new consumer choices. The path of all international business is shaped by external and internal corporate considerations. While there are thousands of international businesses that meet the definition of producer of goods and services over borders, far more intriguing is the study of a select group that in doing business as individual firms altered the nature of economic growth and development. Studies of the history of these companies – and an understanding of what is international business – tell us not only their individual histories but contribute to a fundamental mastery of global economic history in the twentieth century and help explain today's world economy.

Notes

1. This distinction was made in Brian Toyne and Douglas Nigh, *International Business: an Emerging View* (Columbia, SC: University of South Carolina Press, 1997), esp. 27–8.
2. There has long been discussion of the internalization of knowledge within the multinational enterprise. See Peter J. Buckley and Mark Casson, *The Future of Multinational Enterprise* (New York: Holmes & Meier, 1976); Jean-François Hennart, *A Theory of Multinational Enterprise* (Ann Arbor: University of Michigan Press, 1982); Ikujiro Nonaka and Hirotaka Takeuchi, *The Knowledge-Creating Company* (Oxford: Oxford University Press, 1995); and Johann Peter Murman, *Knowledge and Competitive Advantage: the Coevolution of Firms, Technology, and National Institutions* (Cambridge: Cambridge University Press, 2003).
3. In Mira Wilkins, *The Maturing of Multinational Enterprise: American Business Abroad from 1914 to 1970* (Cambridge, Mass.: Harvard University Press, 1974), 412–39, I set up a growth of the firm approach to the development of US business abroad, based on my research on the history of such American companies. The five fundamentals outlined herein were not separated out in that story, but arise from a more general approach to the history of international business, comprising not simply American business abroad and also taking into account the story well beyond 1970.
4. I made this point years ago in Mira Wilkins, *The Emergence of Multinational Enterprise: American Business Abroad from the Colonial Era to 1914* (Cambridge, Mass.: Harvard University Press, 1970), 3; for a more recent elaboration, see Karl Moore and David Lewis, *Birth of the Multinational: 2000 Years of Ancient Business History – from Ashur to Augustus* (Copenhagen: Copenhagen Business School Press, 1999).

5. I feel relatively confident in this generalization, although in prior centuries certain merchants, who also manufactured at home, may well have had partners that manufactured the same products abroad, so this might be called a manufacturer, manufacturing abroad. What occurred in the nineteenth century was however very different. The manufacturer of the goods became the initiator of the international business.

6. In my thinking about these pre-First World War companies and their subsequent history, I have been very influenced by the work of Alfred D. Chandler. What he found on many of these companies domestically, I found true of these companies' international business.

7. Geoffrey Jones has made major contributions on these activities, see especially his *British Multinational Banking, 1830–1990* (Oxford: Oxford University Press, 1993).

8. Most economists believe that profits influence the allocation of resources. One does not have to believe in profit maximization for either a domestic or an international business to accept a key role of profits in resource allocation.

9. British American Tobacco did not, but its precursors American Tobacco and Imperial Tobacco had done so. Also, there were manufacturing companies abroad in the late nineteenth century (not listed in my text), which were not the outcome of a particular business's domestic activities: this was true, for example, of many of the 'free-standing companies' in breweries. On 'free-standing companies', see Mira Wilkins, 'The Free-Standing Company, 1870–1914: an Important Type of British Foreign Direct Investment', *Economic History Review*, 2nd ser., XLI (May 1988), 259–82, and Mira Wilkins and Harm Schröter (eds), *The Free-Standing Company in the World Economy, 1830–1996* (Oxford: Oxford University Press, 1998).

10. Mira Wilkins and Frank Ernest Hill, *American Business Abroad: Ford on Six Continents* (Detroit, Mich.: Wayne State University Press, 1964), 14–19.

11. If certain aspects of this rendition seem to bear resemblance to some of the ideas of John Dunning, the influence is undeniable.

12. *World Investment Report 2003*, 231. This definition is concrete in defining percentages, but vague in terms of what is 'a long-term relationship' and what is 'lasting'. How long-term? How lasting?

13. Economists note the principal, the shareholder, and the agent, the management of the corporation, may have different agendas.

14. On continuities and discontinuities, see Mira Wilkins, *The History of Foreign Investment in the United States to 1914* (Cambridge, Mass.: Harvard University Press, 1989) and Mira Wilkins, *The History of Foreign Investment in the United States, 1914–1945* (Cambridge, Mass.: Harvard University Press, 2004).

15. Tetsuo Abo (ed.), *Hybrid Factory* (New York: Oxford University Press, 1994).

16. These subjects were discussed at a Conference on Ford, 1903–2003: the European History, Bordeaux, 14–15 November 2003 (see Hubert Bonin, Yannick Lung and Steven Tolliday (eds), *Ford: the European History 1903–2003* [Paris: PLAGE, 2003]) and at a Symposium on Hybrid Management, Tokyo, 12 December 2003, convened by business historian Tsunehiko Yui.

17. Robert Boyer, Elsie Charron, Ulrich Jürgens and Steven Tolliday, *Between Imitation and Innovation: the Transfer and Hybridization of Productive Models in the International Automobile Industry* (Oxford: Oxford University Press, 1998), 376. See also Michel Freyssenet, Andrew Mair, Koichi Shimizu and Giuseppe Volpato, *One Best Way? Trajectories and Industrial Models of the World's Automobile Producers* (Oxford: Oxford University Press, 1998).

18. Boyer et al., *Between Imitation and Innovation*, 377.

19. HSBC advertisement in *The Economist*, 29 Nov. 2003.

20. The Singer company was taken over in 1989 by James Ting, a Chinese-Canadian businessman, headquartered in Hong Kong. See *New York Times*, 14 May 1995; *Financial Times*, 3 Oct. 1997 and *Miami Herald*, 5 Dec. 1997. The *New York Times*, 14 Sept. 1999, reported that the Singer company, based in Hong Kong, was (again) seeking bankruptcy protection in the US courts.

21. Wilkins, *The Emergence*, 84–6 (1911 antitrust case). Ranked by foreign assets, BP was number 3, Exxon Mobil number 6 and Royal Dutch Shell number 9, on the *World Investment Report*'s list of the top 100 non-financial transnational corporations in 2001. *World Investment Report 2003*, 187.

22. *World Investment Report 2003*, 187–8.

23. The equity link with American Tobacco was severed with the 1911 US Supreme Court decision; Imperial Tobacco sold its interest between 1975 and 1979, with the final shares sold in March 1980. See BAT Industries, *Facts and Figures, 1991*, 19–21.

24. *World Investment Report 2003*, 188.

25. In 1996, Chiquita Banana captured about 26 per cent of world banana trade (Julian Roche, *The International Banana Trade* [Boca Raton: CRC Press, 1998], 123) compared with some 80–90 per cent before the First World War. It was in bankruptcy again in 2002, re-emerging with a smaller proportion of world trade.

26. Hoover's Online, accessed 29 Dec. 2003, is very useful on the historical sequence in this bank's history.

27. There is a large literature on state-owned companies: see, for example, Renato Mazzolini, *Government Controlled Enterprises: International Strategic and Policy Decisions* (Chichester: John Wiley & Sons, 1979).

28. Richard J. Evans, Introduction to the reprinted 2nd edition (1986) of E. H. Carr, *What Is History?* (Houndmills: Palgrave – now Palgrave Macmillan, 2001), xiv.

9
What is International Business?
A Sociologist's View

D. Eleanor Westney

When Peter Buckley first asked me to contribute to this volume, I agreed with considerable enthusiasm. The actual production of this chapter, however, has been unexpectedly agonizing. 'What is international business?' is a deceptively simple question. Its possible interpretations multiply the longer one contemplates what, in the immortal words of Bill Clinton, the meaning of 'is' is. 'What is IB?' can mean both 'what is the domain of the field of IB?' and 'what should it be?' In addition to the descriptive and normative aspects of the question, one can also conjure up a temporal dimension: What is the field currently? What past developments have shaped it? Where is it heading in the future? And like any academic field, IB can be defined in terms of three related elements: its teaching portfolio, its research domain, and its institutional infrastructure both in the institutional field of the university and in terms of its professional community (especially its professional associations and journals). In short order, a four-word question ramifies into a daunting array of issues.

One gateway to these issues is through personal experience, and if the reader (and the editor) will permit an unacademic first-person account, I shall begin with my own introduction to the question, 'What is IB?' This occurred just over two decades ago, when the Sloan School of Management at MIT was looking for a Japan-focused social scientist to join the International Management group and was willing to hire someone with no expertise in international business and no systematic education in business and management. I have been wrestling with the question, 'What is international business?' ever since.

Personal retrospective

When in 1982 I moved from a position as a Japan specialist in Yale's Sociology department to the two-person International Management group at MIT's Alfred P. Sloan School of Management, the very considerable transition was eased by some unexpected parallels between the fields of Japanese Studies and international business (IB). These parallels have become more apparent in retrospect than they were at the time, but they undeniably shaped my perceptions of IB both then and subsequently.

The fundamental similarity is that both fields are defined by an empirical phenomenon rather than by a particular theoretical perspective. Japanese Studies embraces all things Japanese – culture, polity, society, economy. IB's domain is cross-border business. Therefore both fields are inherently multidisciplinary (though not necessarily interdisciplinary), drawing on a variety of disciplines and paradigms to illuminate the complex empirical phenomenon on which they focus. The field of Japanese Studies has historically centred on language, literature and history, which have constituted a de facto core (not primarily as disciplines but as providers of the basic tools for understanding the phenomenon); it has also embraced the social sciences and the professional fields of law and business. IB draws on the social sciences and on the various fields of management (marketing, operations, HRM, finance, etc.), with, historically, a de facto core focus on the multinational corporation (MNC).

Other similarities derive from this phenomenon-based definition of the domain. Both fields have traditionally demanded of their members a breadth that many other fields have not. A specialist in Japanese sociology in the 1970s, when I was a graduate student, needed both a grounding in the language–literature–history core of the field and an exposure to work on Japan not only in the field of sociology but also in the other social sciences, especially anthropology, economics and political science (at the time, this was a more modest expectation than it was a decade later, when the explosion of research on Japan made keeping simply up in one's own discipline a demanding task). The expectation of breadth was reflected in the teaching portfolio: the basic courses on Japanese society included sessions on perspectives provided by each major subfield of the discipline, such as social change, stratification, family and gender, urban sociology and so on. Thus it was no surprise when the first course into which I stepped upon moving to MIT was called 'International Dimensions of Management', covering the international aspects of the various subfields of business education (marketing, operations, strategy, HRM, etc.). The breadth of the domain, in contrast to the 'mile deep/micron wide' specialization demanded by many other fields, has been an attraction to many of us who joined these fields. However, it has posed problems in an academic context in which legitimacy is conferred on deep expertise and specialization rather than on breadth and integration.

The two fields also both occupied a precarious institutional position, in terms of their place in the university. Each field claims that an understanding of the phenomena it studies is critically important to the portfolio of knowledge and education that its institutional home (the university and the business school) provides, and that claim has generally been recognized by the institutional authorities. However, it has been difficult to translate the recognition of importance into institutional strength. In the Japan field, Japanese specialists at most universities have been scattered across departments (language and literature, for example, in an East Asian Studies department, historians in the History department, and so on). Increasingly, as Japanese money began to fund a growing number of positions in the social sciences and in professional schools in the late 1970s and 1980s, a Japan Studies Centre or Programme provided an umbrella for the specialists hired by individual departments. Despite the deeply held beliefs of those in Japanese Studies that the education and research portfolio of a modern university ought to cover the first non-Western society to become a major global power, however, departments outside East Asian Studies often lacked any deep commitment to maintaining a specialist on Japan – unless the university could generate external funds for the position. IB was in a somewhat analogous position in many business schools. From the early 1980s on, the recognition of the importance of the international dimensions of business has been part of the rhetoric of most business school deans. Most schools have maintained a relatively small IB department or group, and some had International Business Centres or Programmes to link faculty in other departments with an interest in cross-border business. Perhaps surprisingly, however, the widespread rhetoric about the importance of internationalizing business school curricula led in many business schools to debates over whether a separate IB or IM group was really a help in achieving that goal. Many business school faculty outside IB seemed to believe that, like the International Divisions of many major companies, a separate IB department was a transitional (and somehow regrettable) stage on the road to full internationalization, to be replaced as soon as possible by global business units/departments.

Undoubtedly based on the parallel with my experience in Japanese Studies, I have always believed that the most appropriate institutional structure for IB was the maintenance of an IB or IM core group, the 'keeper of the flame', so to speak, without which there was an omnipresent threat that the phenomenon-focused academics would be edged out of other departments by the more narrowly focused discipline specialists. In addition, the core IB group should construct, where possible, a larger umbrella or network to create and maintain linkages among those faculty with a strong interest in the phenomenon but a primary anchor in other management fields (such as marketing or operations). The Japanese Studies parallel does suggest, however, that such an umbrella is more effective when it includes resources to support phenomenon-related research, seminars, and even faculty positions. Like many who enter a new field carrying an implicit institutional model into the new context, I am constantly puzzled that others do not see the obvious advantages of this kind of structure.

The precarious institutional position occupied by both Japanese Studies and IB undoubtedly played a role in their somewhat defensive response in the 1980s to what an outside observer might have considered a welcome development: an explosion of interest in the empirical phenomenon at the core of the field. Japanese Studies witnessed a surge of interest in Japan throughout the 1980s, triggered by Japan's economic success in rebounding after the energy crises of the 1970s and the growing visibility of its manufacturing companies in Western markets. In the case of IB, the rise of cross-border investment and competition in the 1980s, particularly in the Triad of North America, Western Europe and Japan, led to the increasing centrality of global strategy in the Strategy field and growing interest in many other business school departments in cross-border activities (especially in global marketing and global operations management). For both fields, these developments posed the proverbial opportunity and challenge. On the one hand, they validated the importance that each field had long claimed for its phenomenon. On the other hand, although an applied domain is defined by its phenomenon, an academic field is effectively defined by its literature, and in both cases the phenomenon was suddenly being addressed by a rapidly expanding horde of academics who had not steeped themselves in the literature of the field and had no intention of doing so in any systematic way. The fear of losing field-level legitimacy (as opposed to the legitimacy of research on the phenomenon) was not simply a matter of academic turf and institutional position; it also encompassed a very real danger of losing control of and narrowing the research agenda. However, though many of us complained about the invasion of our fields, most responded by taking advantage of the expanded audience for our work and addressed the somewhat instrumental agendas of the newcomers.

In retrospect, I would argue that although both Japanese Studies and IB experienced an upsurge in activity and creativity in the 1980s, in response in part to the explosive growth in interest in their phenomena, both fields paid a price in terms of the critical dimensions of their analyses. To over-simplify considerably, the focus in Japanese Studies on explaining Japanese success and in IB on identifying ideal types and exemplars of the new forms of the MNC and of cross-border business meant giving less weight to long-standing traditions of critical theory in both fields. This left both at a disadvantage when new critical agendas emerged in the 1990s: explaining the sudden and prolonged downturn in Japan's economy in the post-Bubble era in Japanese Studies, and the explosion of interest in globalization in the social sciences, in which IB experts were conspicuous by their absence.

Underlying the ambivalent response to the 'invasion' of both fields by non-specialists is a fundamental dilemma. On the one hand, each field must make a case for the distinctiveness of the phenomenon on which it has built its knowledge base – else how can one justify the existence of a separate field? On the other hand, unless the phenomenon has generalizability to other phenomena and implications for other bodies of theory and research, it is of little or no interest to the more prestigious and powerful domains of knowledge that establish the standards for 'significant' research. With some notable exceptions, such as the work of Ronald Dore (e.g. Dore, 1983) in the Japan field and Mark Casson (e.g. Casson, 1987) in IB, both fields have tended to lean towards emphasizing the distinctiveness over generalizability, at some cost to the contribution each field has made to the underlying disciplines. Trying to balance distinctiveness and generalizability is a constant tension in both fields, and requires both shoring up the professional community and identity and building bridges to other disciplines and fields (for a discussion of this dilemma and an approach to addressing it, see Dunning, 1989).

The professional community and identity of an academic field are reinforced by the professional associations that provide venues for interaction around research and teaching. Professional associations are important agencies for the definition and maintenance of shared professional identity and venues for the cross-fertilization of subfields within a domain. Professional associations tend to be organized on a country or regional basis, but in most fields the largest and the most dominant are those which are centred in the United States, and they draw members from all over the world. In terms of this professional infrastructure, the contrast between IB and Japanese Studies is more striking than the parallel. Japanese Studies has never had its own professional association. Many of the Japan specialists in North America belong to the Association for Asian Studies,[1] and to their own disciplinary association (the American Sociological Association, for example).[2] The AAS reinforces the identity of Japanese Studies as one of a number of 'area studies' fields, and provides links with other Asian specialists that have been of growing importance in recent years, with the expansion of comparative and regional research. Indeed, even within the AAS, Japanese specialists do not have their own governing structure: Japanese Studies is housed within the Northeast Asia Council, which includes Korean Studies, and elections for AAS office are by Council, not individual area. It may well be that the rigours of acquiring a working facility in the Japanese language imprint a shared identity on those in the Japan field of sufficient strength that a separate professional association is unnecessary.

International business, in contrast, has more than one professional association even in North America. The Academy of International Business was founded in 1959, and publishes the leading journal in the field. There is also the International Management division (formally recognized in 1970), within the Academy of Management. The AIB has approximately 3000 members; the IM Division of the Academy has just under 2000 and is the third largest division of the Academy. There is considerable but unmeasured overlap between the two, and sometimes the rationale for two separate structures can be difficult to grasp. However, they do serve different purposes from the viewpoint of professional identity and communication. The AIB aims to bring together those working on cross-border business from the complete range of disciplines and management fields, and provides the IB specialist with a venue for keeping abreast of the entire range of IB research. The IM division of the Academy provides an opportunity for IB specialists to monitor research in their under-lying management fields (other divisions include Business Policy and Strategy, Organization Theory, Organization Behaviour, Human Resource Management, Organization Development and Change, etc.). In other words, the AIB provides networking across subfields within International; the IM Division of the AOM provides networking within subfields across 'mainstream' and International. The benefits of these complementary opportunities are apparently sufficient to compensate for the costs to the field (in time and attention) of maintaining two sets of officers, reviewers and meeting organizers. There may, however, be less visible costs in terms of the resources for building bridges on a community basis (as opposed to the many individual links) with other fields. And there are undoubtedly costs from the fact that, ironically, despite considerable overlapping membership, there is little coordination or cooperation between the two associations.[3]

Looking backward, looking forward

The two decades since I entered the field of IB have witnessed major changes, which are most dramatically illustrated by the changes in the teaching portfolio. In the early 1980s, the Sloan School concen-tration in International Management had three core courses: the basic course on the international dimensions of the business functions that I described above; another basic course called 'International Business Environments' that surveyed different country contexts; and a practicum involving students in team projects in a company engaged in (or aspiring to engage in) cross-border business. I quickly learned that this portfolio represented 'old' IB, and I was fortunate enough to be introduced to the 'new' IB by Chris Bartlett, who at a memorable lunch in 1983 drew and explained the 'Global Integration–Local Responsiveness' framework and its applicability to different levels of analysis (industry, company, function).[4] The teaching of the 'new' IB, focused on the strategy and organization of the MNC, was initiated at Sloan by Don Lessard in the executive education course, and then introduced into the Master's programme. By the second half of the 1980s the teaching portfolio of the IM group had been transformed. Gone was the practicum, on the grounds that its focus on small companies at an early stage of internationalization did not fit the central themes of the field. Gone too was the course on 'doing business in strange places' – after all, the focus of IB was increasingly on the Triad economies. Instead, we offered multiple sections of a core course on the 'new' IB, followed by electives on specific countries or regions (Japan, China, Europe) and on specialized expertise (e.g. International Finance).

Two decades later, the wheel seems to have come full circle. The IM teaching portfolio at Sloan now consists of three basic courses, the two most popular of which are a course on understanding different business environments and a course centred on a team-based practicum (the course on the strategy and organization of the MNC is the third, but it is now in some danger of being seen as the 'old' IB). Of course, the new courses differ in significant respects from their early 1980s counterparts. 'Doing business in strange places' now draws much more systematically on models of comparative capitalism and political economy and much less on models of national culture. The practicum is no longer focused on companies in the New England area seeking to internationalize but unable to afford pricey consultants. Instead, the venues are small firms in other countries (such as Brazil, Italy, New Zealand, Hong Kong) seeking to expand and unable to afford pricey consultants. The course is called 'Global e-lab', and is taught by the IM faculty on the model of the Entrepreneurship Laboratory course (focused on domestic firms) organized by the MIT Center for Entrepreneurship.

One possible explanation of these developments might be that the field took a wrong turn in the 1980s, overemphasizing the large established MNCs and tying IB too closely and exclusively to the field of strategy. However, the fact that IB teaching and research continue to rely heavily on the frameworks and insights of the 1980s is evidence that this explanation would be wrong. Instead, we should recognize that the changes across the two decades and the somewhat surprising similarities between the early 1980s and the early 2000s are a product of the twin engines of change in an applied field like IB: changes in the focal phenomenon, and changes in the paradigms and methods of the underlying disciplines.

In the postwar period through the 1970s, the rapid expansion of firms led the emerging field of IB to focus on explaining why firms internationalized, how they internationalized (organization, modes and processes), and how different business environments affected the why and how of internationalization. In teaching, both for executives and business school students, the last question was often the most interesting. Indeed, in this era the IB classroom was virtually the only place in an American business school that acknowledged the existence of alternative business models and environments. However, in this area of inquiry, IB did not frame distinctive questions or draw on and significantly adapt existing theoretical paradigms, and little of the literature from this era on doing business abroad survives in the IB canon. The contributions to the field from this formative era took the empirical questions of why and how firms internationalized, drew on existing paradigms in other fields to frame the questions and the direction of inquiry, and thereby produced significant conceptual and theoretical advances. To take just one example, for some economists in IB, the question, 'Why do firms internationalize?' became 'Why do MNCs exist?' (which is not the way a sociologist or political scientist would frame the question), an analogy to the economics conundrum of why firms exist if markets are efficient. Buckley and Casson (1976) drew on the work of Ronald Coase to address this question in a way that advanced both the field of IB and the theory of the firm (for more examples of the nexus between empirical phenomenon and theory in IB, see Buckley, 2002).

In the mid-1970s, however, the pace of entry into new foreign markets slowed considerably in many established MNCs (for example, according to Chris Bartlett's 2003 case on Procter & Gamble, P&G entered only one new country in the 1970s). The focus of management attention in the 1970s and well into the 1980s shifted from the challenges of building a presence in new markets to developing more competitive international strategies, reducing the inefficiencies of multiple country-scale operations, and deriving more competitive advantage from dispersed operations. This change in the focus of concern among practitioners was picked up by a small number of researchers at Harvard Business School (C.K. Prahalad, Yves Doz and Chris Bartlett), where contingency theory dominated much of the analysis of strategy and organization (indeed, arguably contingency theory created a new interface between the fields of strategy and organization). The development of the 'Global Integration/Local Responsiveness' framework and the model of the transnational, the major achievements of the IB field in the 1980s, grew out of this combination of the recognition of a shift in the empirical phenomenon and the use of a theory developed in other contexts to frame the key questions and identify new categories and levels of analysis (see Westney and Zaheer, 2001 for a more detailed discussion). Both our understanding of the phenomenon and the theory on which it drew advanced significantly. Indeed, Doz and Prahalad (1993) have argued convincingly that the I/R framework advances contingency theory to the extent that it deserves consideration as a paradigm in its own right.

In the 1990s, in contrast, the fall of the Soviet bloc and the conse-quent opening up of Eastern Europe and Russia, the growth of many emerging market economies, and the increasing receptivity of China and India to foreign investment led even long-established MNCs to resume the rapid expansion of their geographic reach. To use the Procter & Gamble example again, P&G, which in 1980 operated in 27 countries, entered 30 new countries between 1990 and 2000 (Bartlett, 2003). Moreover, entrepreneurial firms in new industries throughout the world were engaging in foreign operations much earlier in their life cycle than had been the case in previous decades. 'Doing business in strange places' again became a central focus of interest among managers and students. This time, however, IB was able to draw on and extend theoretical paradigms in other fields, notably institutional theory in sociology and political science, inter-disciplinary work on comparative capitalism and comparative business systems to address the classic questions of how business environments differ in different locations (see for example Kogut, 1993; Henisz, 2000) and why and how firms go abroad (e.g. Zaheer, 1995; Guillén, 2001), thereby again advancing simultaneously the understanding of the focal phenomena of the field, the conceptual paradigms, and the significance of IB research for other disciplines.

All of this brings us to the most difficult dimensions of the question, 'What is IB?' – what should it be in the future? how should it develop? what nexus of phenomenon and theory holds out the most promising prospect for the advance of the field? One of the few certainties of prediction is that most predictions are likely to be wrong, and it is therefore with considerable trepidation that I advance some prospects for the future – but here they are. The arenas I identify are in the theoretical territory of economic sociology, the fastest growing subfield of sociology over the past decade (see for example Guillén et al., 2002).

The past is an uncertain guide, but it is the best one we have. And the past suggests that the explosive expansion of MNEs in the 1990s will produce an increased interest in how to organize effectively to deal with the complexity not just of scale but also of environments and organizational patterns. Increasingly, MNCs have turned to a relatively new organization design to cope with these complexities: the front/back organization (Galbraith, 2000), in which technology development and production are organized in global business units (the 'back end') and marketing and customer interface are in 'front end' units, in which geography is either the first- or second-order design principle. MNCs are currently wrestling with the coordination challenges of this design, which can probably best be understood and addressed by drawing on recent work in economic sociology and behavioural economics. The unit of analysis in some of this work has been shifting from transactions to interactions and interdependencies, and the classic juxtaposition of market versus hierarchy as a way of governing transactions has given way to the triad of market–hierarchy–network as systems for coordinating interdependencies (e.g. White, 2002). Moreover, economic sociology recognizes these systems of coordination as involving both power and processes of social construction, thereby drawing heavily on the theoretical developments of institutional theory in the 1990s (see for example Fligstein, 2001). Each of the three coordination systems involves different patterns not only of routines and capabilities, but also power and status, interpretation and legitimation. The MNC is therefore extremely promising territory for investigating these coordination systems empirically, because it encompasses all three in its internal operations as well as its interactions with external organizations. In the front–back systems, for example, the interdependencies between the front and the back involve combinations of hierarchy, internal markets, and networks. Framing research questions in terms of these coordination systems can both advance our understanding of the empirical phenomenon and the theoretical paradigms of the underlying disciplines.

A second arena where the nexus of phenomenon and theory holds great promise is the impact of MNCs on the social and political environments in which they operate. This was a major concern of IB in its early years. Indeed, in one of the early textbooks in the IB field, one of the founders of the AIB, Dick Robinson, portrayed the field as being fundamentally a subfield of International Relations (Robinson, 1964). However, in the 1980s and 1990s, the growing receptivity to FDI and the increasing acceptance of the MNC as a force for economic growth, at least among policy-makers, meant that research on the effect of MNCs on the environments in which they operated tended to stagnate. As Ray Vernon (1998) warned, however, the easy assumption that this represented an irreversible advance in the development of MNCs and the thinking of policy-makers is a dangerous one. Growing concerns over the proclivity of MNCs in the late 1990s to expand by acquisition instead of by greenfield investment, concerns over the physical environment and sustainable development, the increasing awareness of MNC managers of the importance of 'non-market strategy' (which often translates into building systematic influence over policy-making), and a growing interest among sociologists in the effects of MNCs on class structure and political systems in developing nations all suggest that MNC managers will face increasing challenges in the next decade. Again, economic sociology provides some concepts for framing research questions, especially in terms of the role of MNCs in the social construction of national and global markets and the social and political role of MNC managers and MNC-affiliated companies in emerging market countries. The concept of industry ecologies, which has a long history in sociology but which is being revitalized in the context of the new economic sociology, provides a framework for lifting debate and research beyond the focus on the 'good or bad' conduct of individual MNCs to more systemic patterns. In particular, the Asian region, with a relatively short experience of market capitalism of the kind taken for granted by Western MNCs, provides an arena for investigating the interface between social and political change and the role and activities of MNCs.

Finally, at the level of the individual–organization interface, an important arena for research is the trend over the last decade for international experience to extend well beyond the expatriate managers who have for so long been the focus of attention in IB. Although they are still important, their numbers (and perhaps their impact) are dwarfed by the horde of middle and lower-level employees sent on short-term international assignments or working on international project teams. Simply mapping this phenomenon and examining the effects on HR systems and policies are daunting challenges for IB scholars. But linking this phenomenon to the complementary theories of human and social capital will do much both to deepen the impact of the research and to build on it to make a contribution to scholarship outside the IB field. Human capital theory has been around for decades; social capital theory has been one of the most active arenas of theory development in the last decade in sociology (for a review, see Portes, 1998). Much of the work on expatriate managers, for example, has been focused on human capital issues: How can an MNC do a better job of selecting expatriate managers and improving their capabilities? What portfolio of expatriate manager profiles best serves the human capital needs of the MNC? Social capital focuses on the networks and influence patterns both of individuals and organizations, and provides a somewhat different framing of the research questions, especially in terms of the negative as well as the positive effects of social capital: for example, what patterns of international experience and exposure produce what levels and kinds of social capital? When do the dominant networks and patterns of social capital make certain shifts in strategy and organization extremely difficult? Social capital is one of the more promising concepts for going beyond abstract concepts of organizational capabilities to disaggregating and operationalizing capabilities, and the MNC is a particularly promising venue for this research, because of the enormous potential internal variety of social capital it encompasses.

In short, IB has flourished in the past when the changes in the empirical phenomena of cross-border business stimulate IB scholars to turn to new sets of theories and concepts (new to IB, though not necessarily to scholarship) and adapt and enhance them in the study of the phenomenon. There is every reason for being optimistic that this process will continue to build the field in the future.

Notes

1. The AAS publishes the interdisciplinary, multi-area *Journal of Asian Studies*, but it contains few articles on Japan and even fewer on contemporary Japan. In 1974, a very strong multidisciplinary Japanese studies group at the University of Washington began publishing the *Journal of Japanese Studies*, a twice-yearly publication that has become the central organ of publication in the field. It is unusual for a field to rely so heavily on a journal published by a single institution rather than a professional institution – but that is not a topic of particular relevance for this chapter.
2. There is often an informal network within the disciplinary association: for example, the Japan sociologists have a networking meeting at the annual meeting of the American Sociological Association.
3. The most recent example of the costs is AIB's decision to move its annual meeting to the summer, putting it on a time frame that coincides with the Academy of Management meetings and creating competition between the two associations for reviewers and papers.
4. I still have the original Bartlett drawings in a somewhat tattered spiral notebook – perhaps a candidate for an e-Bay auction to IB aficionados at some point.

References

Bartlett, Christopher A. (2003) 'P&G Japan: the SK-II Globalization Project'. Harvard Business School case 9–303–003.

Buckley, Peter J. (2002) 'Is the International Business Agenda Running out of Steam?', *Journal of International Business Studies*, 33(2): 365–73.

Buckley, Peter J. and Mark Casson (1976) *The Future of the Multinational Enterprise*. London: Macmillan – now Palgrave Macmillan.

Casson, Mark (1987) *The Firm and the Market*. Cambridge, Mass.: MIT Press.

Dore, R. P. (1983) 'Goodwill and the Spirit of Market Capitalism', *British Journal of Sociology*, 34(4): 459–82.

Doz, Yves, Christopher A. Bartlett and C. K. Prahalad (1981) 'Global Competitive Pressures vs. Host Country Demands: Managing Tensions in Multinational Corporations', *California Management Review*, 23(3): 63–74.

Doz, Yves and C. K. Prahalad (1993) 'Managing DMNCs: a Search for a New Paradigm', in Sumantra Ghoshal and D. Eleanor Westney (eds), *Organization Theory and the Multinational Corporation*, London: Macmillan – now Palgrave Macmillan, 24–50.

Dunning, John H. (1989) 'The Study of International Business: a Plea for a More Interdisciplinary Approach', *Journal of International Business Studies*, 20(3): 411–36.

Fligstein, Neil (2001) *The Architecture of Markets: an Economic Sociology of Twenty-First-Century Capitalist Societies*. Princeton: Princeton University Press.

Galbraith, Jay R. (2000) *Designing the Global Corporation*. San Francisco: Jossey-Bass.

Guillén, Mauro (2001) *The Limits of Convergence: Globalization and Organizational Change in Argentina, South Korea, and Spain*. Princeton, NJ: Princeton University Press.

Guillén, Mauro, Randall Collins, Paula England and Marshall Meyer (2002) *The New Economic Sociology: Developments in an Emerging Field*. New York: Russell Sage Foundation.

Henisz, Witold J. (2000) 'The Institutional Environment for Multinational Investment', *Journal of Law, Economics and Organization*, 16: 334–64.

Kogut, Bruce (1993) *Country Competitiveness: Technology and the Organizing of Work*. New York: Oxford University Press.

Portes, Alejandro (1998) 'Social Capital: Its Origins and Applications in Modern Sociology', *Annual Review of Sociology*, 24: 1–24.

Robinson, Richard (1964) *International Business Policy*. Cambridge, Mass.: Hamlin Publications.

Vernon, Raymond (1998) *In the Hurricane's Eye: the Troubled Prospects of Multinational Enterprises*. Cambridge, Mass.: Harvard University Press.

Westney, D. Eleanor and Srilata Zaheer (2001) 'The Multinational Enterprise as an Organization', in Alan Rugman and Tom Brewer (eds), *Oxford Handbook of International Business*, Oxford: Oxford University Press, 349–79.

White, Harrison (2002) *Markets from Networks: Socioeconomic Models of Production*. Princeton: Princeton University Press.

Zaheer, Srilata (1995) 'Overcoming the Liability of Foreignness', *Academy of Management Journal*, 38(2): 341–63.

10
Epilogue: International Business as an Evolving Body of Knowledge

John H. Dunning

Introduction

After 52 years researching in the field, I did not think I would be asked to write a contribution to a volume entitled *What Is International Business*? But I cannot resist an opportunity to revisit and update some views I expressed in a contribution I wrote in 1988 entitled *Towards an Interdisciplinary Explanation of International Production* (Dunning, 1988), and in my presidential address to the Academy of International Business (AIB) which I gave in October of the same year (Dunning, 1989).

In my thoughts, I have also greatly benefited from reading the earlier chapters of this volume. Towards the end of my own contribution, I will make reference to these as they tell very much the same kind of story to that of my own.

In this chapter, I will first rehearse my own interpretation of the *concept* and *scope* of both 'business' and 'international'. I will then give some attention to the *content* of IB, and how this has evolved over the last two decades; and then go on to suggest a number of (what I perceive to be) critical areas on which, I believe, IB scholarship should especially focus in the next decade. Section 4 then relates my own thoughts to those of the other contributors in this volume. A concluding section of the chapter attempts to draw all these threads together.

Definitions and concepts

Business

The *Oxford English Dictionary*, among others, offers several definitions for the word *business*. Two, I think, are particularly apposite for our purposes. The first is that business is *an enterprise or undertaking which engages in commercial activity*. This I shall refer to as the narrow or *micro* definition of business. The unit of account is the enterprise, firm or corporation. It is primarily a functional and organizational centred definition. It is the one favoured by business scholars; and in this volume, is dealt with most eloquently by Mira Wilkins. The second definition of business is that it is *the activity of commerce, of buying and selling, of purchases and sales, and of transactions and exchanges*. This I shall refer to as the wider or *macro* definition of business. It is a definition favoured by scholars – notably economists – interested in analysing and explaining the determinants and consequences of commercial activity, not only from the viewpoint of the individual enterprise, but also from that of other economic actors, notably national governments, supranational agencies and special interest groups. In the macro definition of business, the unit of account is not confined to business undertaking. More often than not it is a group of firms (e.g. an industry), a region, a country or indeed the world.

Now clearly which interpretation one chooses to take of business – the *organizational* or the *activity* approach – makes a huge difference to the scope of the field of study of (international) business. I personally prefer the second (which embodies the first) as I believe it better identifies business as a body of knowledge or a field of study, which draws upon, encompasses and integrates a variety of disciplinary insights. These insights range right across the curricula of most business schools. In addition, and more recently, IB scholars are increasingly drawing upon the research and writings of their colleagues in business (and economic) history, economic geography, international relations, political science and ethics.

It is, of course, perfectly possible to come near to taking a midway approach between the two interpretations by considering the content matter of the macro definition primarily *from the perspective of the business enterprise*. This suggests that events exogenous to the enterprise, but which affect the goals, strategy and decision taking of its managers, are themselves an integral part of study by business scholars, even though they may not solely or directly address issues relating to the endogenous workings of firms.

I believe this concept of business comes close to that articulated by the editor of *JIBS*,[1] when, in his words, the 'critical signals that will drive the markets for ideas in IB are research across the entire range of topics encompassing the domain of international business studies and theoretical and scientific papers that advance social scientific research on international business' (Lewin, 2004, p. 80).

I also think it reflects the idea that (international) business is essentially an interdisciplinary body of knowledge. Indeed, its uniqueness lies in the fact that the whole of this knowledge is greater than the sum of its separate parts, i.e. by 'internalizing' these parts it adds value to them.[2] While, de facto most IB research will draw upon methodologies of individual disciplines – and these may be published in specialist journals of those disciplines – the comparative advantage of the business scholar is that he or she is aware of the limitations of a single methodological approach and/or seeks to combine his or her own disciplinary training, inclinations and learning experiences with those of scholars from other subject areas. Thus, over the two or three decades, there has been a noticeable and increasing overlapping of the boundaries of, for example, organization and micro-economic theory; of management and industrial economics; of geography, international strategy of firms, of business history and entry modes of cross-border ventures; of corporate governance, ethics and sociology; of cultural studies and international relations, of marketing techniques, and the anthropology of consumer preferences; and of foreign direct investment, corruption and political regimes, to name just a few.

It is my belief that *globalization*, and particularly the cross-border activities of multinational firms, increases the need for more interdisciplinary studies, and that IB provides a useful umbrella for such studies. I also believe that they are primarily issue or activity driven. They are fashioned by events largely outside the control of individual corporations. At the same time, they also require strategists and decision takers within corporations to broaden their views beyond traditional technical issues, for example from those relating to the efficient accessing, creation and utilization of resources, capabilities and markets, to the institutional characteristics and imperatives affecting their behaviour.[3] Nowhere is this better demonstrated than in the increasing attention now being given to relational assets and social capital as components of a country's locational advantages, and to the cultural and ethical content of corporate social responsibility. Both mainstream economists and IB scholars have yet to fully embrace these.[4]

I think that, in the current state of affairs, the wider or macro view of business is currently leading work on these issues. This is because of its innate interdisciplinary characteristics, which globalization has helped emphasize and reinforce. However, in micro business, as demonstrated by the research of both organization theorists and transaction cost economists over the past three decades, issues directly relating to both the comparative advantages of markets and hierarchies as institutional mechanisms, and the specific incentive structures and regulatory regimes which affect the costs and benefits of these alternatives, have been well aired and analysed in the literature.[5]

International business

While in a literal sense *international* – i.e. *between* nations – is not the most apposite word to describe the cross-border activity of economic agents, or the strategy and governance of firms engaged in such activity, I believe that it is a useful generic or threshold term. It can then be extended or fine-tuned to embrace different *degrees* or *forms* of internationalization. Take the *multinational* enterprise (MNE) as an example. The generally accepted definition is that it is an enterprise which engages in value added activity outside its national boundaries. Again, perhaps the term *transnational* is an expression which best describes the nature of the beast. In practice, however, most analysts regard the two terms as interchangeable. But again the threshold definition can be widened or deepened to incorporate different measures of multinationality or transnationality, according, for example, to the number of countries in which a firm produces, and/or the proportion of its global sales or assets derived from outside its home country.

Most recently the word *global* has entered into the business vocabulary. This would seem to suggest that international firms engage in commercial transactions and/or value-adding activities across the globe. Again, de facto, at which point a firm becomes global is bound to be arbitrary. Alan Rugman points out in his chapter to this book that there are few global *multinational* firms in the sense that they engage in value-adding activities in each of the three main regions of the world.[6] However, this is not to say there may not be global *trading* firms – in so far as they source their imports and/or despatch their exports to many countries throughout the world.

In any event, the interpretation of *international* is fairly clear. Whatever the concept – narrow or broad – it comes within the purview of IB. There is, however, one caveat. The definition of international is inevitably, to some extent, contextual in the sense that its coverage can easily change as a result of regrouping of national boundaries, for example the splitting up of the USSR and Yugoslavia on the one hand, and the movement towards a European community on the other. Moreover there are many similarities between the *intra-regional* including clustering activities of firms *within* larger countries, for example China and the USA, and that of the *international* activities of firms *between* smaller countries. This incidentally, is why economic geography and network analysis are becoming such an integral subject of the macro IB studies.

The content of international business (IB)

At any given moment of time, the accumulated (stock) of knowledge and learning capabilities of IB scholars determines the resources and capabilities of IB as an area of study. Together with the incentive and regulatory structures, guiding the motivation and behaviour of teachers and researchers, this determines its *scope* and *content*. This is true of both micro and macro IB scholarly efforts. Such *intellectual* and *institutional* capital may be internally generated, for example via the advance of ideas, methodology, theoretical constructs, analytical techniques, empirical research and policy recommendations. Its direction and scope and interdisciplinary perspective are, however, likely to be influenced by politics, i.e. a reaction to external events and the attitudes and behaviour of the various stakeholders in the global economy. At the same time endogenous generated entrepreneurship, new strategic insights and research within firms may well influence the actions and behaviour of the extra market players, notably governments and supranational agencies and civil society.[7]

In our contemporary global economy such a stock of IB-related assets – and its character – is constantly changing. Over the last two decades, externally events such as technological change, institutional developments, the emergence of new players in the world economic scene, the widening and deepening content of cross-border activity, new organizational forms, regional economic integration, the growth of alliance capitalism and the changing perceptions of the goals of economic development – to mention just a few – have dramatically affected the direction of both micro and macro IB scholarship.

At the same time, since the early 1970s in particular, both the boundaries of IB as a body of knowledge and the depth of understanding and analytical prowess of its scholars and practitioners have enormously advanced. Thirty years ago, the core subjects of micro business largely consisted of economics, management, organization and finance. Indeed, I well remember the early meetings of the AIB, which carved up the individual sessions according to a particularly disciplinary perspective. Today, while these core subjects still provide the essential methodologies and analytical tools to the IB scholar, increasingly, to produce their full value, they need not only to share each others' intellectual capital, but also to draw into their ambit the methodology and techniques of other non-core disciplines, e.g. business history, geography, sociology.

This is even more the case with macro business studies. Any satisfactory analysis of the policy of national governments and the actions of supranational agencies on IB activity ignores the contribution of international political economy and international relations at its peril. The connectivity of economic, social and political agents fostered by globalization is requiring IB as a body of knowledge, to pay more attention to the institutional, cultural and ideological aspects of both the goals of firms and governments, and the means by which the goals can be advanced and its distributional consequences (Dunning, 2004). This is altering the intellectual landscape of both the objectives and content of IB research.

In short, although there are common features of the subject matter of IB studies, for example trade, FDI, portfolio capital movements at a macro level, organizational form, human resource management, marketing systems at a micro business level, the exact configuration of the content of each is likely to be strongly contextual. It is likely to vary across firms, industrial sectors, countries and over time. For example as a mode of communication, e-commerce – and the Internet in particular – was scarcely known in the 1980s. Its widespread adoption has required a new realization of the importance of such virtues as trust, reciprocity, truthfulness and respect for cultural differences. The liberalization of many cross-border markets and the transition of several economies from central planning to market systems has demanded much more attention on the institutional imperatives which underpin efficient markets. A spate of cross-border mergers and acquisitions in the 1990s has required a reconfiguration of the theory of FDI, and also of its consequences to both home and host countries. Global supply chains are now a central feature of any strategic management course, while the importance attached to knowledge capital is requiring modifications to the content of human resource management and innovation-related courses and research projects.

One of the potential strengths of IB as a discipline is its flexibility both to embrace new analytical et al. concepts, and to readily respond to exogenous events and actions. Again, while often no less challenging to the content of the individual disciplines of micro and macro business, the issues frequently need to draw upon knowledge from several disciplines. IB offers (or should offer) a quintessential nexus of interdisciplinary and complementary sets of knowledge and learning experiences. The greater the specialization of subjects, but the more complex the topic of research, the more IB can stake a claim as a useful and unique body of knowledge – and as an avenue for both exploiting the economies of scope of interdisciplinary learning, and minimizing the transaction costs of knowledge creation and exploitation.

Possible future directions of IB scholarship

Some general observations

I have, perhaps, written enough on the common and context specific features of both the boundaries and content of IB. It can be seen that, I believe that, far from it being forced out of existence by the rightful – indeed welcome – embrace of the international dimension by the individual disciplines comprising micro and macro business studies, contemporary external events and recent advances in scholarly research[8] are increasingly pointing to the value of more cross-disciplinary studies. I have suggested that by accessing, creating and utilizing resources and capabilities in different cultures, value systems and institutional norms, that the tackling – let alone solving of any particular IB-related issue – whether it be at firm or at extra firm level needs to more systematically embrace incentive structures and enforcement mechanisms – and the values and belief systems underpinning them.[9]

But let me illustrate further the contextual and networking characteristics of IB scholarship by offering some personal thoughts on what I see to be a few of the externally driven events and actions of the next two decades or so, and also the main actors likely to be involved. Such events or actions, I believe, will enlarge and affect both the content and scope of the micro and macro IB studies – but perhaps most of all the interface between them (as set out on p. 170). But no less importantly, I believe they are all of a nature which will emphasize the value – indeed necessity – of interdisciplinary scholarly approaches to their analysis, empirical examination, explanation and recommendations for action, each of which if properly pursued should enhance the reputation of IB as a body of knowledge.

Each of these events is, I believe, driven by both political and economic trends – not least globalization itself – and also by evolving perceptions and values of the stakeholders in the world economy about what *should be* the central concerns and goals of business activity. I shall briefly consider just three of such issues, namely *poverty*, *security* and *organizational* change. I further believe, along with Witold Heinsz (in this volume) that a useful approach in dealing with these issues divides into the *institutional* which embraces the incentive structures and enforcement mechanisms affecting the motivation and behaviour of the individuals and organizations (including enterprises), and the *technical* which encompasses the resource capabilities and markets of these same individuals and organizations to meet the goals set by them.

Finally, in consideration of these issues, I would like to set them within the framework of what I consider to be the key challenge for IB scholarship of the global economy as it is now evolving. Put in the form of a question it is '*How can society benefit from the advantages of interconnectivity, global economic integration and the reconfiguration and upgrading of global institutions and incentive structures, while at the same time accepting – indeed encouraging, where appropriate – the social, cultural and other valued-laden traditions, which local communities, other interest groups and individuals wish to preserve?'* At each unit of analysis, from the activities of the individuals and corporations to those of governments and supranational entities, and indeed economic systems, this is essentially a paradox of the centrality and subsidiarity of systems, institutions and belief systems. The resolution of the inevitable tensions which flow from it, is, I think, one of the, if not *the* critical issue facing IB and IB scholarly research in the foreseeable future. I shall discuss the agenda of the three issues with this challenge very much in mind.

Poverty

Poverty, in the sense of extreme economic and social deprivation, has always been with us; and most commentators agree that, over the last two decades, more people in the world have been taken out of abject poverty[10] than in any other similar period in history.[11] The problem is, of course, that the population of the least prosperous regions of the world – notably in sub-Saharan Africa – is rising faster than their ability to increase their basic living standards.

At the same time, the industrialized countries in the world have become even richer, with the consequential increase in the absolute income and wealth gap between rich and poor. And it is the perception of this gap, together with the growing awareness[12] of both the poor and the rich about how the other half lives – that this issue is in front of the agenda of the international community. At the same time, the advent of international terrorism, which breeds most potently in the poorest countries, and the perceived sense of economic and social injustice about the distribution of the world's resources and capabilities, and the output of these assets e.g. income, have led richer nations to increasingly accept the need to redress some of this imbalance as a matter of virtuous self-interest.

In a conference on the progress of the Millennium Goals I attended at HM Treasury in London in February 2004, speaker after speaker referred to the real weapons of mass destructions (WMD) not as those which terrorists or rogue states may or may not possess, or be capable of unleashing, but rather abject poverty in the poorer countries of the world (and, indeed, in pockets in some richer countries) and indifference and apathy to the plight of the dispossessed in the wealthier nations. Such huge disparities of wealth breed a sense of social outrage, which, if not satisfactorily tackled by peaceful means, fosters and inflames socially disruptive and, at the extreme, terrorist activities.

International business can play a critical role in helping to reduce poverty. Indeed three of Gordon Brown's plans for the Millennium Goals (Brown, 2004) are directed to IB-related matters. These are: (i) to increase FDI by giving more incentives to the potential investors, (ii) to increase trade by reducing import barriers and export subsidies imposed by developed countries, and (iii) to reduce the volatility and other imperfections in the international financial system. These goals are easier to identify than to attain. To achieve them requires much more cooperation and goodwill both between the governments of developed and developing countries, and among those of developing countries than is at present shown. But the academic, and especially the IB community, also have an important research role and advocacy to play. The elements just described are not just at the heart of international economics. They critically affect both micro and macro IB. They almost all require a holistic approach to development and structural change embracing each of the disciplines of IB. In addition, they encompass many of the issues relating to the determinants and impact of IB activity. They redefine the role played by each of the participants in the globalization process and how they can most fruitfully interact with each other. They dramatically affect the composition of the comparative and competitive advantages of firms and nation states. They require a reappraisal of the interface between incentive structures, and the allocation of resources and capabilities between developed and developing countries. Might then one expect rather more contributions to the IB journals in the next few years on this topic? I very much hope so.

Economic security

If poverty is one of the weapons of mass destruction, the most potent outcome of the social disruption it causes is crime and terrorism. These 'bads' are no longer confined within national boundaries. Globalization has aided the ease and speed at which violent reactions to the gaps between rich and poor can transverse space. As the last few years have shown, the lives of many people and the security of organizations have been either affected or threatened by international terrorism and civil disorder of one kind or another. *Inter alia* these events have led to an upsurge in the value placed on security instruments and devices. At a micro business level, the internationalization of security firms, the need for MNEs to better protect their employees, their value-added activities and their property from terrorist attacks, is likely to demand more attention by analysts. The impact has already been all too evident on transborder transportation costs.[13] At a macro business level, the implications of this form of 'bad' – and the various forms by which its various components may cross space, for example via the Internet, trade, networks, migration and investment – demand more careful examination. As with poverty, this topic also demands an interdisciplinary approach with IB scholars working together with international relations and security experts.[14] *Inter alia* by raising uncertainty, insecurity increases both the production and transactions costs of economic activity. Its opportunity costs, in the form of other benefits forgone, are, potentially, even more serious.

At the same time, the appropriate form of the cross-border organization of these activities and their preferred location may need reappraisal.[15] The events of September 11th and its aftermath, for example, have added a new dimension to the concept of psychic distance and international risk, and are causing MNEs to revise their assessments of particular locations for their value-added activities, and indeed the strategy of their supply chain management. They are also requiring many governments to greatly increase their expenditures on the protection of their constituents, and for supranational agencies to incorporate security issues into their thinking about a whole range of international economic and social issues, notably trade, employee protection, insurance protection and safety measures.

Of the disciplines of IB most likely to embrace security issues into their analysis are financial location studies of business policy and strategic management, the aspects of IB studies deserving particular attention are extra-market incentive structures and enforcement mechanisms – as, for example articulated by Douglass North (1990, 1999) and Oliver Williamson (2002) with respect to border controls (in respect of both people and goods), the formation of cross-border alliances, and investment guarantee schemes.

Again, I ask myself, will the future content of IB teaching and research respond to these cross-border security-related challenges, which seem likely to be with us for at least the foreseeable future?[16]

Multifaceted organizations

The third area of emerging significance which may, I believe, (and should) influence the content of both micro and macro IB studies is the widening constituency of the stakeholders voicing their opinion on global economic and social issues.[17] A review of the articles published in *JIBS* and *International Business Review* (*IBR*) over the last three decades or so reveals that most have either directed their attention to the organization, strategy and operations of MNEs or international trading firms, and that of governments and supranational agencies, or to the global economic environment affecting their conduct, decision taking and policy formation. Only cursory attention has been paid to the role of consumers, labour groups or shareholders in affecting the objectives and behaviour of corporations; and even less to that of civil society (for example as represented by a bevy of NGOs), as it has impacted on the nature and content of global markets, and/or that of the attitudes of, and actions taken by, national governments and international agencies, such as the World Bank and WTO.

Globalization and recent technological and communication advances, coupled with a growing concern among particular interest groups about the perceived inability of traditional institutional mechanisms, namely markets and national governments, to meet, or fully take account of, some of the needs of ordinary men and women (or indeed of the actions of the former where they operate against the latter's interests). This has led to a range of new voices expressing their collective views (and sometimes exercising their combined power) to affect the conduct and activities of business corporations, and the role of extra-market organizations at the bargaining tables throughout the world. Demonstrations by NGO activists from Seattle in 1998 right up to the present day on a wide array of issues are the immediate and most obvious – though not necessarily the most persuasive expression of such concerns.

What are the critical implications of these special interest groups and activists, which range across a spectrum from philanthropic and religious organizations to activists designed to protect or enhance environmental and labour standards?[18] They are threefold. First they are inculcating new, or reprioritizing existing values into traditional business relationships. This is seen in the growth of ethical (e.g. fair trade) buying by consumers, and ethical investment by individual shareholders. This, alongside *top-down* initiatives by governments, with respect to transparency and improved accounting procedures, is prompting a reappraisal of the concept of corporate social responsibility, which, at its very least, is causing businesses to re-evaluate their goals: questions such as 'is profit the only thing shareholders are interested in?' In seeking to achieve legitimate business goals, how far should MNEs take responsibility for employment conditions in poorer developing countries and apropos the distribution of economic rent, to what extent should other stakeholders and governments than shareholders share in the firm's prosperity?

The second is that many NGOs are not only, themselves, engaging in cross-border activities, but, in certain sectors, they are supplementing or replacing those previously undertaken by markets and other extra-market organizations. Examples of such activities include arts, leisure pursuits, and a variety of philanthropic and educational endeavours. Some years ago, it was estimated that the value-added budgets of NGOs accounted for 10–15 per cent of the national income of the USA and UK; and that in 1995 the total labour force of NGOs exceeded that employed by the national government (Salamon and Anheier 1997; Oxford University Press, 2001).

The third impact of civil society on IB activity is through its direct influence on the attitudes and actions of firms, governments and supranational entities, and how these in turn influence micro and macro international business activity. So far attention has been paid to the activities of such organizations, and (to a limited extent) how they have affected the behaviour of other IB-related organizations. But there has been very little rigorous examination of the economic or business implications of their activism; or how such activism has affected (or if implemented could affect) the institutions of global capitalism, such as, for example, the composition and content of the WTO's deliberations, the scope and activities of MNEs, the policy framework of national governments, and the philosophy and actions of the World Bank.

Yet, in so far as they are becoming a more important part of or influence on IB activity, each of these three dimensions surely requires more extensive and careful assessment by both micro and macro business scholars. Moreover each interacts in various ways with the other. Several organizations are working with, or seeking to influence, business perceptions and behaviour with respect to poverty. It is also increasingly recognized that extreme poverty and economic (in)security are inextricably linked and that to tackle them, both a multifaceted and coordinated approach is needed. There is also a more realistic appreciation that, with the growing complexities of the globalizing economy, a more holistic approach to the challenges and opportunities of both micro and macro IB is necessary. This, in turn, necessitates a deeper and more rigorous study of the institutions underpinning successful coalitions, cross-border partnerships and networks both within individual organizations and between organizations.

These challenges and opportunities are likely to be most pronounced when business operations transcend cultural and ideological boundaries. Cultural studies have always been a part – but a fairly self-contained part – of the IB curriculum. In the coming years, I believe they need to be an integral part of each and every aspect of IB teaching and research, as they critically influence the micro and macro incentive structures which determine the content and success of IB activity.

Some comments on the contribution to this volume

I fully acknowledge that my choice of three of the most significant topics likely to affect the content of IB in the next decade or more is both personal and selective. I have, for example, given no attention to area or industry studies. Apropos the former, I believe both India and China will become a focal point of IB studies; while research into the determinants and consequences of knowledge and institutional intensive service-related activities is likely to grow. Considering the value chain of MNEs, I would foresee innovating, outsourcing and marketing activities playing a more important role. Cross-border clustering, both within regions and across national boundaries (e.g. in Europe, North America and Eastern Asia) is likely to command more attention, as indeed is the whole issue of regional and global governance. New forms of the governance of international agencies – and the scope of their activities – are also likely to be explored.

However, to conclude this brief Epilogue I would like, very briefly, to relate my reflections to some of the points made in the earlier chapters of the volume, each of which I thought was perceptive, incisive and of real practical value.

To begin with Mark Casson's reflective and discerning contribution, I fully concur that the health of IB scholarship, in part at least, rests on its visionary perspective. Paraphrasing the Bible,[19] 'Without vision, IB as a body of knowledge, may perish!' However, this vision, as Mark acknowledges, needs to be multifaceted. Partly it rests on methodology and analytical rigour; partly on content – should not IB be paying more attention to macro business, and the global economic? system; partly about the likely future of entrepreneurship and institutions; and partly on the disciplines involved.

Apropos the latter reason, as an economist, I particularly welcomed the chapter by Eleanor Westney, and the plea she makes for a more definitive contribution of economic sociology and human capital theory to our identification of new challenges for the IB scholars. In particular she identifies three of these. The first is to do with the coordinating challenges of new organizational designs to cope with the complexity of the global operations of MNEs, and the interdependencies of the institutions in which they are embedded. The second is the extent to which the concept of industrial ecologies might help us better understand the extent to which the cross-border operating experiences of MNEs, particularly with reference to human resource management, might add to our knowledge about how best to access and utilize social capital. The third is the growing attention now being paid to the role of relational assets and social capital, and the systemic patterns of MNE behaviour that might be influenced, or influence, institution variants of market-based capitalism.

I also appreciated the important distinction made by Daniel Sullivan and John Daniels between the *human* and *scientific* dimensions of IB, and also the reference by Withold Heinsz to the institutional voids in IB. Withold's concluding insights that IB research should incorporate recent findings from the relevant disciplines on the nature of the institutional environment resonates strongly with my own views. I also concur with Steve Kobrin, that information, knowledge and advances in learning capabilities will continue to be the main source of wealth creation over the foreseeable future. However, I also believe that it will be the extent and quality of the interaction between these assets and the human environment in which they are embedded – not to mention the incentive mechanisms, values and belief systems underpinning both – which will be the critical determinant of the success or failure of economic globalization. In Steve's closing words 'avoiding dysfunctional globalization will require a world economy that is both more equitable (in terms of distribution) more pluralistic (in terms of organization of its component national units) and some form of global governance; international institutions which are both effective and legitimate' (p. 54).

Taking a more micro business stance, Mira Wilkins, in her chapter in this volume as in her many other writings, identifies the IB firm, as first and foremost, an institutional structure; and her innovative discussion of the concept of hybridization is essentially to do with incentive structures and enforcement mechanisms affecting the strategy and behaviour of firms.

While Alan Rugman and Alain Verbeke predominantly take a resource-based view to explaining the changing spatial dimension of MNEs, in several places in their chapter they acknowledge the importance of both corporate and country (or region) specific institutionally related variables. Indeed, in their analysis of the regional concentration of MNEs, they specifically acknowledge the transaction cost variables which link or meld the more institutionally related ownership advantages of firms with those of the countries or regions in which they operate. They also hint at the need for a wider and more varied business agenda for studying the role of both MNEs and extra-market actors in affecting the form of, and response to, regional integration.

Bruce Kogut too, in his usual perceptive manner, focused on the unique characteristics of IB. He regretted not only the loss of micro IB related topics to the individual business disciplines, but thought that some of integrative and holistic character of IB had been compromised in the process. At the same time, he criticized the IB literature for 'losing its engagement in the world'. 'Are we asking the right questions' he asks? If, in the language of Herbert Simon, IB is a field of architectural design, would it fall? Possibly not, but its foundations are certainly shaky. As I read both Bruce's and other essays, I sense that IB must reconcile the benefits of trying to establish universal verities within that of contextual distinctions. (This incidentally is precisely the paradox likely to challenge students in trying to assess the costs and benefits of globalization and global capitalism over the next two decades.)

Conclusions

I sense that the overwhelming conclusion of the chapters in this volume is that IB is still not making the best use of its comparative advantage as a unifying and holistic body of knowledge of several interrelated disciplines. Whatever the reasons for this in the past, it would seem that the particularly distinctive characteristics of globalization are offering IB a second chance – a new opportunity in Ed Safarian's words – to be a new 'field in ferment' offering new 'institutional focus and methodological accessibility' (Safarian, 2003). This is because, in posing the challenge of how best to reconcile the benefits of integration and harmonizing cross-border business activities with those of the specific economic, social and cultural objectives and needs of particular countries and/or interest groups, the role of values, incentive structures and regulatory regimes in fashioning and influencing the global and regional human environment in which micro and macro IB operates, inevitably requires taking an inter-disciplinary perspective.[20]

In various ways, each of the contributors to this volume both acknowledges this challenge, and offers useful suggestions on how scholarly research and teaching may respond to it. But as Bruce Kogut puts it, the challenge does not rest just with IB as a body of knowledge, but on how it can perform its integrative tasks in the context of the worship of the golden calf of academic specialization and tunnel dogma currently prevalent in many business schools and in some functional disciplines. Perhaps, more than in other areas, this is where the need for Mark Casson's concepts of romantic and analytical – not to mention moral – visions most need to be applied.

My final point, to which I think there is a general consensus, is that the content of IB is continually evolving and is likely to do so – possibly at an increasing pace and in several different directions – over the foreseeable future. More than anything else, the technological and spatial characteristics of globalization are requiring IB scholars to reappraise the ingredients of their subject matter and their research priorities, methodologies and teaching practices.

To our intellectual qualities each of us needs both a sense of vision and a flexibility in mindset. We need, too, our own store of institutional capital – which affords us an acknowledgement of the value of our chosen area of study, and the internal incentive structures which makes us proud to give it of our best. To end on a personal note, IB has been good to me over the last five decades. As long as I continue to write, and to share with students and younger scholars my knowledge and learning experiences, I shall certainly try to further enhance both my intellectual and institutional capabilities.

Notes

1. See, for example, the editorial by Arie Lewin in Volume 35 Issue 2 of 2004.
2. In my presidential address (Dunning, 1989) I likened the coordination of the disciplines making up IB to that of the firm coordinating its core assets with those of other firms (and in so doing lowering the transaction costs of doing so via the market). IB as a body of knowledge adds value to its constituent disciplines in exactly the same way.
3. For a review of the current state of institutional economics and its relationship to IB theory see e.g. North (1990, 1999), Williamson (2002), Mudambi and Navarra (2002) and Maitland and Nicholas (2003).
4. But see Dasgupta and Serageldin (2000) and Dunning (2004).
5. See, for example, several essays in this volume notably those by Peter Buckley, Mark Casson, Jean Francois Hennart and Eleanor Westney, Srilata Zaheer and Bruce Kogut, in Rugman and Brewer (2001).
6. The Americas, Europe and Asia and the Pacific.
7. As consultants, business school scholars may well influence the strategy and behaviour of individual enterprises. National governments usually have a bevy of economic advisers, while the writings of individual scholars have almost certainly influenced the ideas and philosophy of supranational organizations, e.g. Joseph Stiglitz, in the case of the World Bank, John Williamson and Barry Eichengreen in the case of the IMF, and John Stopford and myself in the case of UNCTAD.
8. As for example set out in Dunning (2001).
9. I have tried to explore how this might be done with respect to the approach which IB theorists might take to economic (and social) development (Dunning, 2004).
10. Defined as an income of $1 or less per day.
11. According to World Bank figures, although, in 1998, one-fifth of the world's population lived on less than $1 a day the proportion of the population in developing and transition economies receiving such low incomes fell from 28.3 per cent in 1987 to 24.0 per cent in 1998. Most of this decline took place in East Asia and the Pacific (World Bank, 2001, p. 23).

12. Made possible through travel, the Internet, TV., etc.
13. As a direct result of September 11th, for example, it was estimated that air freights rose by 10 per cent (OECD, 2002).
14. For some recent contributions on the economics of terrorism and its consequences, e.g. for crisis management, military spending and the implications for trade, investment and cross-border business logistics, see OECD (2002) and Gold (2004).
15. Thus, for example, countries which offer the best protection from social disorder or disruptive activities are likely to attract more FDI; while in venturing into unfamiliar territories, the efforts of MNEs to minimize the effects of such 'bads' might best be advanced by their forming joint ventures with local communities.
16. Since this chapter was written a new edited volume dealing with some of the implications of terrorism for the international business environment has been published (see Suder, 2004).
17. Sometimes referred to as multi-stakeholder initiatives (MSIs). For a recent discussion of how such initiatives are shaping the agenda in respect of corporate social responsibility, and particularly the relationships between MNEs and extra-market organizations, see UNRISD (2004).
18. There are literally thousands of NGOs some of whom engage in activities outside their national boundaries. See e.g. Oxford University Press (2001) and Falk (2003).
19. Proverbs 29: 18.
20. I only came across Oded Shenkar's excellent contribution to this debate after I had completed my chapter. But I so much agree with his view that the competitive advantage and added value of IB lies in the synergetic combination of global and local knowledge that is unavailable to and not imitable by its major competitors, in particular economics and strategy (Shenkar, 2004, p. 161).

References

Brown, G. (2004) 'Making Globalisation Work for All. The Challenge of Delivering the Monterrey Consensus. Speech given at HM Treasury, London, 16 Feb. 2004 (www.hm-treasury.gov.uk).

Dasgupta, P. and I. Seralgeldin (eds) (2000) *Social Capital: a Multifaceted Perspective*. Washington, DC: The World Bank.

Dunning, J. H. (1988) 'Towards an Interdisciplinary Explanation of International Production', in J. H. Dunning, *Explaining International Production*, London and Boston: Unwin Hyman, 306–26.

Dunning, J. H. (1989) 'The Study of International Business: a Plea for a More Interdisciplinary Approach', *Journal of International Business Studies*, 20(3): 411–36.

Dunning, J. H. (2001) 'The Key Literature on IB Activities 1960–2000', in A. M. Rugman and T. L. Brewer (eds), *The Oxford Handbook of International Business*, Oxford, Oxford University Press, 36–68.

Dunning, J. H. (2004) 'Towards a New Paradigm of Development. Implications for the Determinants of International Business Activity'. Reading and Rutgers Universities, Mimeo.

Falk, R. (2003) 'On the Political Relevance of Global Civil Society', in J. H. Dunning, *Making Globalization Good: the Moral Challenges of Global Capitalism*, Oxford, Oxford University Press, 280–300.

Gold, D. (2004) *Economics of Terrorism*. New York, Columbia International Affairs. On line Case Studies, March 2004.

Griffiths, B., J. O'Neill and M. Buchanan (2003) 'Globalisation and the Challenge of Reducing World Poverty', London, Goldman Sachs, Global Economics Paper, No. 94, 8 July.

Lewin, A. Y. (2004) 'Letter from the Editor', *Journal of International Business Studies*, 35(2): 79–80.

Maitland, E. and S. Nicholas (2003) 'New Institutional Economics: an Organizing Framework for OLI', in J. Cantwell and R. Narula (eds), *International Business and the Eclectic Paradigm*, London and New York: Routledge, 47–73.

Mudambi, R. and P. Navarra (2003) 'Institutions and International Business: a Theoretical Overview', *International Business Review*, 11(6): 635–46.

North, D. (1990) *Institutional Change and Economic Performance*. Cambridge: Cambridge University Press.

North, D. (1999) *Understanding the Process of Economic Growth*. London: Institute of Economic Affairs.

OECD (2002) 'The Economic Consequences of Terrorism', *OECD Economic Outlook*, 71: 118–40.

Oxford University Press (2001) *Global Civil Society Yearbook*. Oxford: Oxford University Press.

Rugman, A. E. and T. Brewer (2001) *The Oxford Handbook of International Business*. Oxford: Oxford University Press.

Safarian, A. E. (2003) 'Internalization and the MNE: a Note on the Spread of Ideas', *Journal of International Business Studies*, 34(2): 116–24.

Salamon, L. M. and H. K. Anheier (1997) *Defining the Non-Profit Sector: a Cross-national Analysis*. Manchester: Manchester University Press.

Shenkar, O. (2004) 'One More Time: International Business in a Global Economy', *Journal of International Business Studies*, 35(2): 161–71.

Suder, G. G. S. (ed.) (2004) *Terrorism and the International Business Environment*. Cheltenham: Edward Elgar.

UNRISD (United Nations Research Institute for Social Development) (2004) *Corporate Social Responsibility and Development: Towards a New Agenda*. Geneva: UNRISD.

Williamson, O. (2000) 'The New Institutional Economics: Taking Stock, Looking Ahead', *Journal of Economic Literature*, XXXVIII, September, 595–613.

World Bank (2001) *World Development Report 2000/2001. Attacking Poverty*. Oxford: Oxford University Press.

Index